Incentivizing For-Profit Investment in the Non-Profit Initiatives of The Community Cooperative:
An Evaluation Study

by

Dr. Norman Keith White, Esq.

A Dissertation Presented to the
FACULTY OF THE USC ROSSIER SCHOOL OF EDUCATION
UNIVERSITY OF SOUTHERN CALIFORNIA
In Partial Fulfillment of the
Requirements for the Degree
DOCTOR OF EDUCATION

December 2020

ACKNOWLEDGEMENTS

To my dissertation committee chair, Dr. Jennifer Phillips, for being a stern but guiding hand and inspiring me to constantly define my position instead of defending my biases. Thank you for believing in me and being so supportive that I would often feel unworthy of your help. Your care for my work provided a foundation for the confidence I have going forward. My time in your care and under your guidance has made me a better professional, a better student and a better human. Thank you and I am forever grateful. Cartier, Lauren and Natalie- I love and appreciate you folks so much.

To my dissertation committee members, Dr. Helena Seli and Dr. Kalima Rayburn, for challenging me to be produce the best version of myself through my work and for encouraging me in the belief that my work is important. Your expertise and guidance has helped me refine my lofty but ever-present goal of changing the world. Thank you both for working with me and on me as I developed in this program. Thank you!

Completing this dissertation would be impossible without the support of my incredible wife, Allegra, and our children, Kennedy, Kalle, Klark, Kingston and Kohen. This dissertation and all of the efforts to create a more sustainable world are dedicated to my family. I love you Allegra, and I owe my growth and development to your love, patience and faith. Thank you for choosing me.

To my best friends, Mom and Dad. Norman, Sr and Gloria White. I've always used my middle name (Keith) in an effort to establish my own identity, but as I've grown that identity is more established in how you raised me. You provided incredible examples of love, grace, faith and perseverance. And although I am also using a pseudonym for my last name (Africa), it is an effort to honor the ancestors that chose you to be my parents. I could not have asked for better parents. I love you. And that's on periodt!

To my Brooklyn Combine family, you guys saved my life in a time when I was lost and looking for community. I love you guys. Now let's disrupt up the world!

TABLE OF CONTENTS

LIST OF TABLES

LIST OF FIGURES

ABSTRACT

This qualitative study evaluated the steps necessary for a non-profit organization to incentivize private investment in its non-profit initiatives. The research questions for this study examined the knowledge, motivation and organizational factors that influenced the Community Cooperative's efforts to incentivize private investment in its non-profit initiatives. The research methods included interviews with the Board of Directors of the Community Cooperative and a document review. The researcher received unanimous approval by the Board of Directors to conduct the study and gained approval through school leadership and the university's Institutional Review Board.

The data analysis produced several themes. These themes were that the Board of Directors possessed procedural knowledge gaps and self-efficacy motivational gaps. Additionally, the organizational settings did not provide enough structural support or accountability. Without enough structural support and accountability, the organization could develop ideas but failed to execute on those ideas. These themes were exhibited by the stakeholders' inability to collect data and create programming that incentivized private investment in its non-profit initiatives.

Recommendations included allocating resources towards the development of programming and data collection that incentivize private investment. The other recommendation includes providing training for the stakeholders in the organization so that they learn how to execute the steps required to achieve the organizational goal.

CHAPTER ONE: INTRODUCTION

Introduction of the Problem of Practice

This dissertation addresses the need to incentivize private investment in non-profit initiatives and the challenge of finding shared common goals when private institutions support non-profit entities. Non-profit institutions can be very effective when the institution can develop community programs that are both in alignment with their non-profit initiative and attractive to private investors. When different institutions share common goals and desired outcomes, the financial support of one institution into another with the mutual expectation of a benefit in return, is considered an investment. Grabenwarter and Heinrich's (2011) research and inability to find many shared common goals between private institutions and non-profit initiatives illustrates this problem and is an example of the challenges that exist in solving this problem. The concept of private investment in non-profit initiatives creates a unique opportunity for non-profit entities to offer a return on investment that is not limited to an interest rate. However, the evidence shows that positive social impact and other non-profit outcomes are not enough to incentivize private investment in non-profit and government work (Shaoul et al., 2011). Thus, the work of non-profit entities involves providing a return on private investment that is directly connected to a social good and also financially competitive with traditional investment scenarios. These returns could be in the form of tax credits that make development for the benefit of underserved communities profitable or the creation of workforce development programs that provide jobs to vulnerable communities and skilled labor to employers. By framing the funding of non-profit work as an investment, a non-profit can increase the potential for program underwriting and scale to serve the increasing needs of underserved populations. This problem is important to address because private investment in non-profit and governmental work is essential to building strong and sustainable communities (Roundy et al., 2017).

Organizational Context and Mission

The Community Cooperative for Progressive Action, Inc. (pseudonym, The Community Cooperative) is a non-profit organization dedicated to sustaining the culture that supports and advances the well-being of oppressed peoples in general, and the Pan-African diaspora in particular. To this end, the Community Cooperative works with schools, community organizations, and dedicated city officials to help provide critical education, leadership, and social support programs to youth and young adults in low-income and under-served communities. The Community Cooperative is deeply impacted by its inability to incentivize private investment because the organization currently relies on the donations of its community members, the board, and grant applications. These sources of funding place limitations on the Community Cooperative because grants are often limited to a specific government or foundation initiatives that may not be in alignment with the Community Cooperative's values or goals. As an organization with an annual operating budget of $125,000, two part time contractors and nine volunteers, the Community Cooperative is stretched to capacity as it serves approximately one thousand local residents of Brooklyn through three different initiatives. Since the work of the Community Cooperative is focused on marginalized communities, the members of the community have limited funds to support the organization and Board Members do not have the capacity to sustain the financial needs of the organization.

Organizational Goal

The Community Cooperative's goal is to achieve at least thirty percent of its funding from private investment that fulfills a community need by the end of 2021. This goal was set after recognizing the importance of private investment in non-profit initiatives. The theory behind this goal is that for-profit investment creates an expectation of accountability while gifts rarely create accountability measures for organizational or systemic gains (Greller, 2015). The ideal type of investor that the Community Cooperative would seek to attract would be a developer seeking infrastructure and programming for a housing initiative like Gotham Developers, Inc., a large employer seeking workforce development like Amazon, or a quasi-government organization or agency seeking to provide services to a marginalized community like Safe Horizon.

Community and workforce development data are attractive to potential private investors that are tasked with partnerships with local governments while social engagement is attractive to investors seeking brand promotion opportunities. To this end, the organization is committed to developing programming that can be memorialized and exhibited for potential investors to show that the organization's programming will provide a return on investment as well as remain consistent with the organization's non-profit initiatives. Additionally, the organization is committed to developing data collection methods that exhibit the effectiveness of the organization's programming in community development, workforce development and social engagement.

Related Literature

This literature review will examine the research on private investment into non-profits and government work. It is important to note that this review is not an examination of the research on charitable giving or philanthropy, but instead, specifically looking at private investment in non-profit work that has a positive social impact and a financial return. By examining how for-profit institutions choose their investment in vehicles of positive social impact, this section will identify the corresponding metric for success. This examination will review the problem of finding shared desired outcomes and goals between private institutions, non-profit organizations, and government agencies. Following the general research literature, later sections of the study will examine the Clark and Estes Gap Analysis Framework (2008) and, specifically, the knowledge, motivation, and organizational influences on a non-profit's development of programming and initiatives that incentivize private investment.

When private institutions struggle to find shared common goals with non-profit entities and the governments they support, society has trouble building strong and sustainable communities (Hanleybrown, Kania, & Kramer, 2012). Trelstad and Katz (2011) asserted that for-profit institutions and non-profit entities often have very different goals when conducting business. The researchers found that specifically, for-profit companies usually have a goal of increasing corporate profits while non-profit companies usually have a goal of solving a social problem. Brest and Born (2013) researched this issue and found that while most investments that seek a social impact produce market rate returns, an investor seeking to produce social impact must be willing to make financial sacrifices in order to contribute to the market.

There are few private institutions willing to invest in initiatives with small profit margins and fewer examples of private institutions willing to absorb the risk associated with investing in non-profit and government work. While there is on-going debate in the financial industry on the definition of an "impact investment," there appears to be a consensus that an impact investment is a capital investment intended to create positive social impact beyond financial return (Jackson, 2013). Wood, Thornley and Grace (2013) posited that while tax subsidies and other incentives exist for institutions to impact invest, private institutions are still reticent to invest in non-profit or government initiatives without clearly established and identifiable profit incentives. Positive social impact alone is often not enough to incentivize private institutions to invest in non-profit and government work because impact investing is predicated upon the belief that there are shared values between non-profit purposes and for profit entities (Bugg-Levine & Emerson, 2011). Finding confluence between asset owners, asset managers, demand-side actors, and service providers is an initial step towards solving the problem of incentivizing impact investing (Jackson, 2013). Private profit versus social impact as competing goals is not a new area of conflict, however, the struggle to find common goals and values at their points of intersection is a new discipline in a rapidly developing society.

Impact investing is distinguished from simply offering tax-deductible donations because donations come with a lower level of accountability and expectation (Milligan, & Schöning, 2011). Milligan and Schöning's (2011) research showed that impact investments are designed to drive innovation and provide returns on investment that are directly aligned with social good while donations typically provide no requirement of proficiency or community development.

Importance of the Evaluation

Evaluating how non-profit entities incentivize for-profit investment is important because finding shared common goals between non-profit entities and for-profit institutions is essential to solving real world problems like the achievement gap in under-served communities and the growing global wealth disparity (Forrer, Kee, Newcomer & Boyer, 2010). To this end, evaluating how the Community Cooperative incentivizes private investment in its organizational initiatives will help the organization understand how it can become a sustainable institution that helps to solve problems without only relying on the goodwill of donations. The problem of finding shared common goals when private institutions support non-profit entities and government work is important to address because private institutions, non-profit entities, and government agencies are all stakeholders in the success and sustainability of society (Forrer, Kee, Newcomer & Boyer,

2010). If the Community Cooperative can develop effective partnerships with for-profit entities to provide resources to their service population while also returning a profit to these partners, a mutually beneficial relationship will be fostered that will allow the Community Cooperative to scale its model. These types of partnerships are essential because the social and ecological path that society is on is unsustainable because private profit and wealth often comes at the expense of social good (Arrow, Dasgupta, Goulder, Mumford & Oleson, 2010). The growth of private wealth and public poverty is broadening the divide of humanity (Arrow et al, 2010).

One example of where a for-profit company and a non-profit company partnered is explored in the Trelstad and Katz (2011) research. The Trelstad and Katz (2011) research discussed how malaria nets were developed and showed how private and public partnerships can effectively solve problems and increase private profits. In this research, a non-profit entity partnered with a for-profit company to provide malaria nets during an outbreak of malaria (Trelstad & Katz, 2011). This partnership ended the malaria outbreak and provided a profit boon to the for-profit entity (Trelstad & Katz, 2011).

The Community Cooperative has an opportunity to assess its strengths and weaknesses as well as evaluate its knowledge, motivation and organizational influences on this goal of incentivizing private investment. Solving public problems with private investment is a progressive way to close achievement gaps, poverty gaps and racial gaps that have previously been informed by purposeful class divides perpetuated by corporate drive for profit. If these problems are not solved, there will be a widening divide in humanity, draining of natural resources and the continued journey towards an unsustainable future (Crifo & Forget, 2013). This evaluation will assess The Community Cooperative's proficiency at incentivizing private investment while remaining true to its core values and non-profit initiatives. The importance of this evaluation will be underscored by evidencing the Community Cooperative's effect on positive community development while providing a return on investment to a for-profit company for its investment in the same non-profit initiative.

Description of Stakeholder Groups

A stakeholder group is a group of individuals who directly contribute to and benefit from the achievement of the organization's goal. The Board of Directors of the Community Cooperative is a stakeholder group in the Community Cooperative. The instructors are also a stakeholder group in the Community Cooperative as staff members and instructors play an integral role with the computer coding courses offered by the organization. The participants and students are a stakeholder group in the Community Cooperative as students in the computer coding and photography workshops offered by the organization.

The Board of Directors at the Community Cooperative are responsible for creating the mission, vision, and focus of the organization. An important task in establishing a mission is identifying a purpose. The Board of the Community Cooperative are tasked with providing a purpose for the mission and inspiring a passion for the vision. By clearly communicating the purpose, mission, and vision of the organization to its members and society at large, the board is establishing the core values of the organization. Consistent with the core values of the organization, the board has developed an organizational goal of incentivizing private investment in the Community Cooperative. The Board of Directors developed this organizational goal by looking at what progressive steps would be necessary for the organization to scale. While resources were identified as a necessary component of growing the organization, partnerships were identified as the main component to any sustainable growth. The Board determined that for-profit institutions would be better partners than other non-profits who would also compete for grants and funding. They also determined that two programs would not be enough to incentivize private investment. The board also reasoned that creating more than three programs would create management and accountability issues outside of the organization's capacity. Using this reasoning, the Board chose to develop three programs in an effort to incentivize private investment. In order to track progress toward the goal, the Board set three-month and six-month goals for programming initiatives that would align with the organization's overall goal.

The instructors at the Community Cooperative are responsible for adhering to and promoting the core values of the organization. This work includes instructing members of the community on coding, self-advocacy, financial literacy and legal process. By developing strong skills in the community that they serve, the instructors at the Community Cooperative are promoting the core-values of the organization.

The participants in the workshops and services provided by the Community Cooperative embody the core-values of the organization by carrying the work forward in their respective communities. While the participants come from various age groups and capabilities, the community goal is to develop proficiencies in skills that enrich their personal lives as well as their community. The participants range in ages as low as 11 years old to early 30's (though there have been senior citizens trained in coding), and as community stakeholders, develop skills that can benefit their communities. Attendance by participants ranges from 25-30 participants per week with males making up approximately 65% of each session.

Stakeholder Group for the Study

Although a complete analysis would require participation from all stakeholder groups, for practical purposes, this study will focus on the Board of Directors. This stakeholder group was most instructive in analyzing this organizational goal since this goal was set by the Board of Directors. The Board of Directors of the Community Cooperative are also tasked with working in programming and fundraising as well as promoting the services of the organization. These tasks give the Board a first-person view of the proficiencies and needs of the Community Cooperative. Additionally, this stakeholder group has the most influence in the process that is required to achieve this organizational goal. The Board of Directors are important to the process of achieving the organization's performance goal because the Board sets the benchmarks for formative assessments that indicate whether the organization is on target to meet its goal. Failure to remain on task and meet each intermediary goal will jeopardize the Board's goal to develop three programs that incentivize for-profit institutions to invest in their non-profit initiatives by the February 2021. With the development of effective programs that provide data indicating proficiency in workforce development, social service support and youth and student programming, the organization would seek to meet with private investors seeking to impact invest in non-profit initiatives. These private investors would be partners in community development, restorative justice and coalition building while also providing examples of the profitability of impact investing. See Table 1.

Table 1

Organizational Mission, Global Goal and Stakeholder Performance Goals

Organizational Mission

To support and advance the well-being of oppressed peoples in general, and the Pan-African diaspora in particular. To this end, The Community Cooperative works with schools, community organizations and dedicated city officials to help provide critical education, leadership, and social support programs to youth and young adults in low-income and under-served communities.

Organizational Performance Goal

The Community Cooperative's goal is to achieve at least thirty percent of its funding from private investment that fulfills a community need by the end of 2021.

Board of Directors Goal	Instructors/Staff Goal	Students/Participants Goal
The Board of Directors will develop three programs that incentivize for-profit institutions to invest in their non-profit initiatives by February of 2021.	The Instructors and Staff of the organization will implement the programming by June of 2021.	Students and participants will become proficient in areas of instruction and provide feedback loops to staff and the Board that prove the effectiveness of the instruction and programming.

Purpose of the Project and Questions

The purpose of this project is to conduct a needs' analysis in the areas of knowledge and skill, motivation, and organizational resources necessary to reach the organizational performance goal. The analysis will begin by generating a list of possible needs and will then move to examining these systematically to focus on actual or validated needs. While a complete needs analysis would focus on all stakeholders, for practical purposes the stakeholder to be focused on in this analysis is the Board of Directors. The questions that guided this study are the following:

1. What are the Board of Director's knowledge and motivation related to incentivizing private investment in non-profit initiatives?

2. What is the interaction between organizational culture and context and Board of Directors' knowledge and motivation to increase private investment in non-profit initiatives?

3. What are the recommendations for organizational practice in the areas of knowledge, motivation and organizational resources related to private investment into non-profit initiatives?

Methodological Framework

To answer these research questions, the project employed a qualitative method of data gathering and analysis of knowledge, motivation and organizational context (Clark & Estes, 2008). Additionally, the project used descriptive methods to provide contextual background into the knowledge, motivation, and organizational context (McEwan & McEwan, 2003; Stringer, 2014). Using interviews, the research explored the Board of Directors' capacity and willingness to develop programming that incentivizes for-profit investment in non-profit initiatives. This framework and these research methods were instrumental in understanding the knowledge and motivation of the Board, as well as organizational influences. This research also provided understanding into the culture of the Community Cooperative as an organization, how it developed and how it can improve.

Definitions

Donation: a gift given from one party to another with no expectation of repayment.

Impact Investment: an investment that has an expected yield of return that includes a social good that is tied directly to the investment.

Social Responsible Investment: an investment that expects a lower yield of return than a traditional investment because of its focus on social good.

Non-profit company- an organization that has been granted tax-exempt status by the Internal Revenue Service because it furthers a social cause and provides a public benefit.

For-profit company- a business or organization whose primary goal is to make money or profit.

Organization of the Project

While this first chapter provided an outline of the problem associated with incentivizing for-profit investment into non-profit initiatives, the second chapter will provide a literature review as well as frame the knowledge, motivation, and organizational influences necessary to develop solutions to this problem. Chapter three of this dissertation will provide the methodology for conducting the research and obtaining the qualitative data of the Board of Directors from the Community Cooperative to provide further context to the problem of practice and the corresponding proposed solutions. In chapter four, the data compiled will be examined, assessed and analyzed. Finally, chapter five will provide data-based solutions to the problem of divergent institutional goals and the challenge of creating business synergy between non-profits and for-profit entities.

CHAPTER TWO: REVIEW OF THE LITERATURE

Influences on the Problem of Practice

Procuring private investment in non-profit work is challenged by differing desired institutional outcomes and missions. This chapter examines the knowledge, motivation and organizational influences necessary to develop shared common interests and partnerships in profit-making and social good.

The History and Development of Private Sector Investment

While the Private sector has historically focused on increasing profit margins, recently, there has been an increased focus on the process of economic development as distinguished from economic growth. Economic development is different from the concept of economic growth in several ways. While economic growth is tethered to macroeconomic conditions and market forces, economic development represents the conditions that determine the microeconomic functioning of the economy, affecting both the quality of inputs and the opportunity set for firms (Feldman, Hadjimichael, Lanahan & Kemeny, 2016). Economic growth is a quantifiable measure while economic development is a qualitative measure (Feldman et al, 2016). Economic growth is quantified by an increase in value while economic development is focused on quality improvements, risk mitigation, innovation, and entrepreneurship that place the economy on a growth trajectory (Feldman et al., 2016).

Because economic development has broader implications for economic growth, the private sector has increased its focus on creating more opportunities for development (Feldman et al, 2016). The Feldman (2016) article indicates that this includes looking at what forces are beneficial or adverse to development through private institutions, social capital, labor and capital mobility, and income and wealth equity. Gordon (2010) asserted that current economic development rates are the slowest in measured American living standards over any two-decade interval recorded since George Washington became president. Cowen (2011) has described the last several decades by coining the phrase, "the Great Stagnation." With these concerns and the growing belief that economic development is the best solution for sustainable economic growth, the industry has been focusing on the microeconomic foundation of the economy (Feldman et al, 2016).

The Cingano (2014) article makes a strong case for focusing on sustainable economic development as a method to increase economic growth. Relying on data from the Organization for Economic Cooperation and Development, an intergovernmental economic organization with 36 member countries, Cingano (2016) asserted that income inequality, inequity and lack of community development have a negative and statistically significant impact on subsequent economic and community growth. Further, policies to reduce income inequalities should not only be pursued to improve social outcomes but also to sustain long-term economic growth (Cingano, 2016). It is also essential that these policies promote equality of opportunity and access to quality education because promoting employment for disadvantaged groups through active labor market policies, childcare supports and in-work benefits are foundational to economic development (Cingano, 2016).

The United Nations' work in creating sustainable development goals has been highlighted in the Assembly (2015) article where UN Secretary-General Ban Ki-moon created initiatives aimed at economic development. By creating Sustainable Development Goals (SDGs), the United Nations has prioritized development that focuses on creating partnerships with the private sector in support of sustainable development and problem solving at the local, national and global level (Assembly, 2015). These examples of increased private sector and government focus on sustainable development are consistent with the growing belief that economic growth is untenable without development that is informed by non-profit goals.

The Standard Goals of Private Investment

Traditionally, the principle goal of private investment is to yield the highest margin possible. The history of private investment for-profit investment in the West is complicated by the development of industrialism and the partnership between governments and profiteers in the Caribbean (Fichtner, 2014). Fichtner's (2014) study indicates that while private profiteers were once celebrated, a shift developed when society began to develop global initiatives aimed at sustainability. With a view towards globalism and sustainability, investment vehicles needed to provide profit margins, spur tax revenues and improve quality of life (Fitchner, 2014).

In order to accomplish increasing goals and desired outcomes, the financial markets needed to develop additional methods of investment. With increased methods of investment, private equity funds can reap the benefits of economic development (Metric & Yasuda, 2011). The Metric and Yasuda (2011) article describes how the increase in economic development diversified the pool of potential investors and more importantly, increased the pool of global problem solvers. This growth in the pool of investors spurred economic growth. This supports the ideology that opening access to the private investment market drives profit margins (Gutiérrez & Philippon, 2017). In their study, Gutiérrez, and Philippon (2017) note that when less people and entities have access to the competitive market, profit margins decline. Consequently, the results of this study indicate that providing equity in access to the market will improve profit margins (Gutiérrez & Philippon, 2017).

The Changing Landscape of Investment Goals and Models

With the development of multiple major global crises, sustainable social good has often become an additional goal in private investment. For example, core investment and banking activities suffered a steep decline following the recession of 2008 (Wójcik, Knight, O'Neill & Pažitka, 2018). While large U.S. banks remain dominant globally, they have experienced the biggest declines in revenue in contrast to Asian banks that have capitalized on the growth of local markets (Wójcik et al, 2018). This reliance on local markets is based on the belief that developing gross domestic product is a useful metric to measure potential for capital growth (Wójcik et al, 2018). While not abandoning the principles of globalism, investment tools that remain global in scope but local in focus are yielding returns provide sizeable profits as well as measurable social good. The Wójcik (2018) study illustrates how gross domestic product is developed by programming that addresses the financial and social welfare of a region or community.

Any discussion about private investment without some discourse on the effects of capitalism is incomplete. To be clear, capitalism has had a negative effect on the environment, humanity and the concept of fair trade (Soederberg, 2009). However, local initiatives and non-profit programming have provided marginalized groups with an opportunity to have a voice. Partnerships between non-profit organizations, local communities and private investors have created unique opportunities for holistic development of local communities and cities at large (Soederberg, 2009). The Soederberg (2009) article asserts that any regression back to strict entrepreneurialism is a return to the private profiteering of the Caribbean and will provide no positive effects on sustainable practices or economic development.

Businesses around the world are beginning to commit resources to measuring and reporting on the wider impacts of their activities beyond financial performance (Shinwell & Shamir, 2018).

Shinwell and Shamir's (2018) research asserts that this commitment to corporate social responsibility (CSR) and understanding and reporting social and environmental impact is good for business. The connection between environmental variables, social developments, business performance and various financial outcomes (such as stock-market performance, profits, etc.) has been extensively documented over the last few decades (Shinwell & Shamir, 2018). A study by Clark, Feiner and Viehs (2015) in partnership with Arabesque Partners found that sound sustainability standards lower companies' costs and raise their profitability. According to the same analysis, a company's stock-market activity is positively influenced by sustainable practices (Clark et al, 2015).

Improved measurement and reporting on the impact of investment on people's well-being is also being driven by investor demand (Shinwell & Shamir, 2018). The research shows that investors are becoming more concerned with the environmental, social and governance (ESG) performance of firms when building their portfolios (Shinwell & Shamir, 2018). Accordingly, an increased value is being placed on environmental impact, stakeholder relationships and whether the company meets basic ethical standards concerning the company's leadership and management (Shinwell & Shamir, 2018). This transition towards sustainability has been largely internal and based on market factors, however, investors are not the only entity pressuring businesses to pay more attention to their wider impacts and to become more socially and environmentally responsible (Shinwell & Shamir, 2018). More recently, consumers have been demanding more responsible conduct from corporations and private, while using their consumer choice to influence the behaviors of the business community (Shinwell & Shamir, 2018).

The Standard Model of Non-Profit Development and Funding

Historically, non-profit entities have not held an agenda to create profits or enrich businesses or individuals. The Robinson (1996) articles supports the position that the primary purpose of most non-profit entities is to perform a service of social good. The standard practice for most non-profit entities is to rely on grants and donations to staff their organizations and run the programming of these organizations (Robinson, 1996). Using grants from government agencies and philanthropic donations from businesses and individuals, non-profit organizations typically provide social good services at cost (Robinson, 1996).

As the landscape for fundraising has developed and been influenced by private market volatility, non-profit organizations have placed an increased focus on their organizational sustainability and the changing needs of their complex operating environments (Al-Tabbaa, Gadd, & Ankrah, 2013). With increasing pressure to achieve best practices in performance and ensure their continued sustainability, non-profit organizations have been compelled to develop new methods of fundraising to support their programming (Cairns, Harris, Hutchison & Tricker, 2005). This is underscored by a growing need for non-profit organizations to provide services for their targeted populations and also the increasing requirement by governmental funders to ensure that the recipients of their financial support (i.e. the non-profit organizations) have the organizational capacity to deliver services effectively (Eisinger, 2002). These factors require non-profit organizations to run efficient programs while also being proficient in business development that provides for scale (Lecy, Schmitz & Swedlund, 2012).

Lecy, Schmitz and Swedlund (2012) article posit that non-profit organizations must have a business model in operation that creates enough working capital or revenue to keep the entity's business running in order to be sustainable. More recently, effective practices have taken on additional urgency among non-profit entities due to more specific demands for accountability, transparency, and financial responsibility (Lecy et al, 2012).

Emerging Practices in Non-Profit Funding and Development

Herman and Renz (2008) suggest that the credibility and stability that are crucial to the development of a non-profit organization can be measured by several traits. These traits include comparative practices, multi-dimensional practices, effective management practices and a commitment to best practices limited in scope and focus. As the marketplace for executives becomes more competitive, non-profits are forced to compete against for-profit organizations for talented staff (Carnochan, Samples, Myers & Austin, 2014). Additionally, non-profits have growing accountability mandates from funders and government partners because performance measurement data has proven helpful in establishing proficiency and efficacy (Carnochan et al, 2014).

Some researchers have expressed concern over the association between non-profit organizations and their reliance on funding to provide advocacy (Kimberlin, 2010). According to the theory of Resource Dependency, non-profit organizations receiving revenues from funders face pressures that may adversely affect their ability to effectively advocate or provide services (kimberlin, 2010). In an effort to address these concerns, many non-profit entities have begun to seek alternative methods of fundraising, including soliciting investments from private entities, entering partnerships with Private Investors, providing fee-based services and procuring government contracts (Aulgur, 2016).

Challenges in Incentivizing Private Investment in Non-Profit Initiatives

Incentivizing private investment in non-profit initiatives requires capturing data and creating programming that further the organizational goal. Capturing data that incentivizes private investment requires collecting data that will show an alignment in values or goals between the non-profit initiative and the private investor. Creating programming that incentivizes private investment will require the execution of programs that produce shared desired outcomes between non-profit initiatives and private investors.

Capturing Data that will Incentivize Private Investment into Non-Profit Initiatives

Non-profit entities are often required to provide quantitative data projecting competitive returns in order to incentivize partnerships with private entities or in order to procure private investment (Klijn & Koppenjan, 2016). The partnership between governments, for-profit investment and non-profit service providers has been defined as public-private partnerships (PPPs). The development of PPPs has become more common in an effort to improve public service delivery and for large infrastructure projects that are meant to incentivize private sector investors to use their skills to partner in the production of better services (Klijn & Koppenjan, 2016). PPP's allow governments to provide accountability to private sector partners through sanctions in order to ensure against opportunistic conduct (Klijn & Koppenjan, 2016). Additionally, PPP's allow governments and private sector partners to hold non-profit partners accountable for efficacy and proficiency by the shortening or lengthening of contracts and resources.

Private investors consider public-private partnerships as exercises in impact investing (Chowdry, Davies & Waters, 2014). Impact investing is distinct from other forms of investing or socially responsible investing because impact investing requires the return on investment to be specifically tethered to a social good (Chowdry et al, 2014). The Chowdry, Davies and Waters (2014) article identifies challenges with impact investment when projects are financed with external capital and private investors choose to under invest in social good. Under investment arises when an investor does not completely internalize the social value of a public good (Chowdry et al, 2014). In an effort to remedy the challenge of under-investment, many PPPs have developed Social Impact Guarantees that set a minimum threshold for problem solving and measurable social good (Chowdry et al, 2014).

The Kharas and McArthur (2014) article posits that non-profit partners in impact investment models will likely need more ambitious financing for strategy development that can mobilize increased public, private and mixed financing. In arguing that public-private partnerships must be constructed at a fine level of disaggregation in order to have an impact, the Kharas and McArthur (2014) article also asserts that non-profit organizations will need to be increasingly ambitious. Many private investors have expressed a desire for more effective public-private partnerships that create a framework within which they can participate more effectively in profitable, development-oriented investments (Kharas & McArthur, 2014). The development benefits from investments made by for-profit partners include increased tax revenues, increased employment rates, the expansion of access to social services and the innovation and cost competitiveness that for-profit partners can generate.

Tying Investment to Programming

In order to successfully procure private investments, non-profit entities will need to tie the investment directly to programming that will provide measurable returns that are connected to social good (Warner, 2013). Non-profit initiatives and entities can attract private investment to social programs by paying a market rate of return if predefined outcome targets are met (Warner, 2013). The importance of collaboration among philanthropy, government, and the investment community is supported by the available research on this topic (Ragin & Palandjian, 2013). Tying investment to social impact invites new way to advance public-private partnerships and introduce innovative financing solutions to scale proven social programs (Ragin & Palandjian, 2013). Impact investing ignites greater funder interest in evidence-based practices in social service delivery, government interest in performance-based contracting and impact investor appetite for investment opportunities with both financial returns and social impact (Ragin & Palandjian, 2013).

The Ragin and Palandjian (2013) article suggests that the popularity of impact investing has grown exponentially in recent years. For example, the article describes how the Rockefeller Foundation and others have prioritized addressing complex societal problems requiring larger scale funding and greater collaboration among philanthropists, government, and private investors (Ragin & Palandjian, 2013). Although impact investment only represents a small proportion of the total assets under private investor management, these assets represent a substantial and growing pool of capital that can fund programs to solve societal problems (Ragin & Palandjian, 2013).

Many impact investors share the common goal of finding projects that provide social impact and generate a financial return (Ragin & Palandjian, 2013). The community of impact investors is broad, diverse and includes investors seeking to support a variety of projects in both developed and emerging markets (Ragin & Palandjian, 2013). These markets include areas requiring development in affordable housing, accessible health care, financial services for the poor, and clean energy (Ragin & Palandjian, 2013). The desired financial returns may range from below-market to risk-adjusted market rate returns, while investments may take the form of equity, debt, credit enhancement, or instruments that combine a mixture of all of these elements (Ragin & Palandjian, 2013). These mixtures may include program development-related investments or mission-related investments (or both), in which, unlike grants, foundations require a high level of confidence in the return of finances (Ragin & Palandjian, 2013). Diversified financial institutions, pension funds, high-net-worth individuals, and fund managers may also make impact investments, in addition to foundations (Ragin & Palandjian, 2013).

A study by Bhattacharya, Oppenheim and Stern (2015) suggests that the world is in the midst of historic structural transformation. Major changes are occurring globally in an effort to attain the sustainability and equity standards that the world is setting for itself practices (Bhattacharya, Oppenheim & Stern, 2015). As major expansion of investment in modern, clean, and efficient infrastructure will be essential to attaining the growth and sustainable development objectives, non-profit organizations can properly position themselves to participate in this development with progressive business practices (Bhattacharya, Oppenheim & Stern, 2015). The expansive financing needs of problem solving projects can only be met through effective non-profit governance and the mobilization of private financing to non-profit initiatives (Bhattacharya, Oppenheim & Stern, 2015). The pool of private capital attracted to solving societal problems is growing (Bhattacharya, Oppenheim & Stern, 2015). The current stock of $3–4 trillion in public finance projects held directly by private investors and entities has the potential to grow in excess of $15 trillion over the next 11 years in ways that could improve overall portfolio performance (Bhattacharya, Oppenheim & Stern, 2015).

The Clark and Estes Gap Analysis Framework

Clark and Estes (2008) provide a framework for understanding organizational and stakeholder goals by identifying and analyzing gaps that exist between each level and each goal. The framework examines stakeholder knowledge, motivation, and organizational influences and how these criteria inform performance gaps (2008). The four types of knowledge and skill used to determine if stakeholders are proficient in reaching performance goals are factual, conceptual, procedural, and metacognitive (Krathwohl, 2002). Some motivation influences are the value placed on achievement of goals, the choice to continue working toward the goals and the mental effort and desire to accomplish the goals (Clark & Estes, 2008; Rueda, 2011). Self-efficacy, attributions, values, and goals are motivational principles that can be considered when analyzing the performance gaps (Rueda, 2011). Additionally, Clark and Estes (2008) asserted that organizational culture, resources, and processes should be considered when examining organizational influences on stakeholder performance.

These elements of Clark and Estes' (2008) gap analysis will be examined in the context of the Board of Director's knowledge, motivation, and organizational needs to meet their performance goal of developing programming that incentivizes private investment in the Community Cooperative's non-profit initiatives. The assumed influences on the Board's performance goal in the context of knowledge and skills will be discussed in the first section. The Board's motivation to accomplish their goal will then be examined in the next section. Finally, organizational influences on the achievement of the Board's goal will be examined. In Chapter 3, these stakeholder knowledge, motivation, and organizational influences will be examined through the methodology that is also discussed in chapter 3.

Stakeholder Knowledge, Motivation and Organizational Influences

The following review of current scholarly literature and research focuses on the knowledge, motivation, and organizational influences required for the Board of Directors (Board) of The Community Cooperative to achieve their stakeholder performance goal. The performance goal for this group of stakeholders is to create programming with measurable performance benchmarks that will incentivize private investment into the Community Cooperative's non-profit initiatives by February 2020.

Knowledge and Skills

The application of knowledge is necessary for the Board, which governs the Community Cooperative, to meet their performance goal. Knowledge provides this group of stakeholders with an opportunity to engage in monitoring and self-assessment of their efficacy prior to program development, during program development, and after implementation of subject programming (Baker, 2006). In order to develop the programming to meet organizational goals, the Board will need to develop critical problem solving skills that will address future challenges (Clark & Estes, 2008). Being able to meaningfully organize and connect new knowledge to prior knowledge is essential to this process (Schraw & McCrudden, 2006). Thus, knowledge assessment is the first critical step in gap analysis to determine if stakeholders have the knowledge and skills needed to achieve their goal.

The identification and examination of knowledge influences, knowledge types, and assessment methods is fundamental to identifying gaps and achieving performance and stakeholder goals. Rueda (2011) and Krathwohl (2002) identified the four types of knowledge as factual, conceptual, procedural, and metacognitive. Factual knowledge is based on the foundational aspects of information that are specific to domains, disciplines, activities, and terminology (Rueda, 2011). A basic understanding of these terms is required in order to solve problems within this framework (Krathwohl, 2002). Conceptual knowledge is an understanding of concepts, principles, theories and categorizations required for understanding issues (Rueda, 2011). Procedural knowledge is the knowledge of process and refers to an individual's knowledge of how to accomplish a task (Rueda, 2011). Metacognitive knowledge is an individual's knowledge of their self, their own thinking and cognitive process (Krathwohl, 2002; Rueda, 2011). Krathwohl (2002) posited that metacognitive knowledge helps an individual understand why they might act and when they might act in a certain way.

Based on a review of the current literature, three primary knowledge influences of the Community Cooperative's Board will be discussed and categorized into one of the previously identified knowledge types. Understanding the knowledge types is instructive in determining the appropriate assessment for each knowledge influence of the Board. Obtaining effective assessments of the Board's knowledge will be foundational in the examination and analysis of the stakeholder goal.

Understanding the Value of Private Investment in Non-profit Initiatives

In order to achieve their performance goal, the Board will need to have conceptual knowledge of the factors that incentivize private investment in non-profit initiatives. This knowledge influence is conceptual because it emphasizes proficiency in identifying and understanding concepts, constructs, and contexts. Private investment provides viability to non-profit initiatives and social caché to social movements. Having conceptual knowledge of the relevant factors informing private investment into the Community Cooperative will inform the Board's necessary steps to accomplish the organizational goals. These organizational goals shall inform the tasks to be performed by the Board.

The Board's development of programming that focuses on institutional analysis of data and societal returns will create a culture of growth and accountability (Cardoso, Meireles, & Peralta, 2012). Through case studies on scale and sustainability, Trelstad and Katz (2011) were able to compare the mission of non-profit organizations, the mandate of government initiatives, and the margins of for-profit companies along with how each of these intersect. This series of qualitative case studies was used to examine where private and public partnerships intersect and have shared common goals or values (Trelstad & Katz, 2011). This examination of common goals between the non-profit sector and for-profit business gives stakeholders valuable information to develop programming that renders metrics that inspire private investment.

In 2015, Hacke, Wood, and Urquilla conducted a quantitative study of the chief motivating factors of private investors. Through a series of surveys and interviews, investors revealed what inspired or informed investment and how investment was distinctly different from philanthropy. This insight and conceptual knowledge could only be developed with a thorough understanding of the different connections involved in investing and how they relate to corresponding non-profit goals. Understanding or creating the congruence between non-profit initiatives and private investment will prove instructive since the Board will be making management decisions for the organization, and, to a larger extent, creating precedent in the non-profit and social justice area of practice.

Develop Programming and Assessments that Attract Private Investment

The second knowledge influence that the Community Cooperative's Board needs to achieve their performance goal is to know how to develop programming and assessments that attract private investment. This knowledge influence is procedural knowledge as it emphasizes how to do something. Specifically, this knowledge influence emphasizes the program development, assessment, data collection, and analysis to meet the stakeholder goal successfully. The research of Wilson, Bunn and Savage (2010) indicated that in order to incentivize private investment, non-profits are required to provide data that substantiates expected return that is independent of social good. Any comprehensive development of programming that attracts private investment will be informed by extensive field notes, in-depth interviews, and explanatory case data that creates a framework for private investor stakeholder collaboration (Wilson, Bunn, & Savage, 2010).

The Wilson, Bunn, and Savage (2010) study employed a comprehensive analysis of social partnerships among a complex network of stakeholder organizations. This quantitative study used field-notes from 33 in-depth interviews and a mix of inductive and deductive reasoning to formulate a conceptual framework and research propositions for a private-public social partnership (Wilson et al., 2010). Through the use explanatory case data, this research developed a framework of stakeholder collaboration in a complex setting involving a mix of for-profit and non-profit organizations (Wilson et al., 2010). This conceptual framework offers an in-depth understanding of private-public partnership development and relationship dynamics and the procedures necessary to carry out the partnership (Wilson et al., 2010). These public and private collaborations are often structured so that each partner is tasked with a goal that is consistent with their respective focus (Loxley, 2012). Loxley's (2012) research provides an example of how public private partnerships evolved following the global financial crisis of 2008 to meet the needs of municipalities and the surrounding business and social interests. By partnering private interests with congruent public organizations and identifying their shared interests in solving problems, Loxley's (2012) research shows that for-profit institutions can solve problems while addressing their desire for positive profit margins.

Assess and Develop Board Proficiency in Program Development and Data Collection

The third knowledge influence that the Board needs to achieve their performance goal is assessing and reflecting on their ability to develop proficiency in program development and data collection that incentivizes private investment. This knowledge influence is categorized as metacognitive knowledge because the focus is on the stakeholders' ability to self-reflect and assess their own understanding and abilities. Lanier (2018) posited that self-reflection inspires emotionally intelligent leadership. Emotionally intelligent leadership is the cornerstone of a stable environment where sustainability and innovation hallmarks of success (Lanier, 2018). Stakeholder reflection requires the Board to assess what they do well and to reflect on where there are opportunities to improve their performance.

The research of Torfing, Sørensen, and Røiseland (2016) indicated that stakeholder reflection is a healthy step towards driving non-profit innovation and partnerships. Further, stakeholder reflection allows the Board to learn from initiatives that did not work and improve on initiatives that were successful. Consequently, the Board of Directors of the Community Cooperative need to assess their ability to develop proficiency in program development and data collection. Effective programming and data collection will be a storytelling tool provided to investors that explains the work, benefit and potential impact and return that can be gained by investment. Papineau and Kiely's (1996) research supports this position by asserting that the process of evaluation and reflection are foundational to strong and empowered stakeholders. By engaging in a comprehensive process of reflection and assessment, the Board of the Community Cooperative can confidently approach performance gaps with data and analysis. Table 2 categorizes the three knowledge influences by knowledge type, assessment methods.

Table 2

Knowledge Influence, Knowledge Types and Knowledge Assessments

Knowledge Influence	Knowledge Type	Knowledge Influence Assessment
The Board of Directors need to understand what factors incentivize private investors to invest in non-profit initiatives.	Conceptual	Interview Board Members and ask them to paraphrase the importance of the value of private investment in non-profit initiatives. Use publicly available items that require respondents to identify, classify or categorize principles, or interpret, compare theories, concepts and principles.
The Board of Directors need to know how to develop programming and assessments that attract private investment.	Procedural	Interview Board Members and ask them to explain how to develop programming and assessments that attract private investment.
The Board of Directors need to assess and reflect on their ability to develop proficiency in program development and data collection that incentivizes private investment.	Metacognitive	Interview Board Members and require them to provide the methods they use to become proficient in program development and data collection.

Motivation

While knowledge-related influences are a study on the Board's ability to know what is necessary to achieve performance goals, a study on motivation-related influences will examine the Board's desire to achieve the identified performance goal (Rueda, 2011). Motivation-related influences present additional critical considerations that are essential to the Board achieving their performance goal. Motivation is the primary measure of a stakeholder's desire to undertake a task and achieve a goal (Mayer, 2011). While motivation and knowledge are closely related, motivation-related influences are very different from knowledge-related influences as knowledge related problems cannot be solved with motivation-based solutions and motivation related problems cannot be solved with knowledge based solutions (Clarke & Estes, 2008). Along with knowledge and organizational barriers, the authors identify motivation as a necessary factor in performance assessment. Increasing motivation increases performance and helps the institution achieve organizational goals (Clark & Estes, 2008).

A comprehensive analysis of how motivation informs performance is an important process in determining what an organization needs in order to be sustainable or scale (Rueda, 2011). Six theories of motivation within cognitive psychology include (1) self-efficacy, (2) value, (3) interest, (4) attributions, (5) goals, and (6) emotions (Clark & Estes, 2008; Mayer, 2011; Rueda, 2011). The authors assert that each of these theories contribute to three behavioral measures of motivation. These behavioral measures are choice, persistence, and mental effort (Clark & Estes, 2008; Mayer, 2011; Rueda, 2011). Choice provides a measure of what is valued based on the choices made the stakeholder. The level of persistence is determined by the resilience of the stakeholder and provides a measure of the stakeholder's determination. And the amount of mental effort applied to a problem will be a direct result of the level of motivation of the stakeholder. The following sections will discuss value and self-efficacy as the critical measures in evaluating the Board's motivation to achieve their stakeholder goal.

Expectancy Value Theory: Task Value

In 2006, Eccles posited that motivation is driven by two fundamental questions: "Can I do the task?" and "Do I want to do the task?" The first question is a question of self-efficacy while the second question is a question of expectancy value (Eccles, 2006). Expectancy value theory is based on the belief that there is importance and utilitarian value in the task that is undertaken by the stakeholder and the likelihood that the behavior will have a successful outcome. The more value that a person places on a task, the better likelihood that the person will apply themselves to completion and proficiency in that task (Rueda, 2011). A stakeholder with complete faith that they can accomplish a task will commit to completion of that task.

In Bear, Rahman and Post's (2010) study about the impact women have on a Board's focus on corporate social responsibility (CSR), the value that the Board of Directors placed on an initiative directly influenced the allocation of resources to that initiative. This study focused on a single organization and how this value influenced the Board's critical function of monitoring management (Bear, Rahman & Post, 2010). If the Board does not place a high value on an initiative, the Board may not work as hard to deliver the required resources or hold management accountable for tasks necessary to successfully complete an initiative. This illustrates how important it is for the Board to value an initiative that an organization is trying to complete. In McMurray, Pirola-Merlo, Sarros, and Islam's (2010) study on the effect that leadership has on the organization's climate and over-all wellbeing, the research was definitive in asserting that leadership is essential to an organization accomplishing any stated goal. This study examined multiple organizations with the research suggesting that the Board of an organization controls the climate of an organization and an ecosystem that is amenable to an initiative will be vested in the success of that initiative (McMurray, Pirola-Merlo, Sarros, & Islam, 2010). Alternatively, if a Board does not create a climate that is amenable to an initiative, the initiative will likely fail (McMurray et al., 2010).

Self-Efficacy Theory

The second motivational influence impacting the Board is self-efficacy. The Board of Directors must believe they can meet the performance goals of obtaining private investment through the relevant tasks that are required to reach performance goals. Self-efficacy is a social cognitive belief based on people's perceptions of their own abilities to complete a task (Bandura, 1997). The more a person believes that they can achieve a task, the more motivated that person will be to overcome obstacles and achieve the task (Rueda, 2011; Clark & Estes, 2008; Pajares, 2006). Several factors that have an effect on self-efficacy include experience, observations of others, input from others, and emotional or psychological reactions (Pajares, 2006; Rueda, 2011). The research indicates that self-efficacy increases with success and decreases with failure. This affirms the assertion from Pajares (2006) that experience is very influential in the self-efficacy of an individual. The self-efficacy factors apply to individuals as well as group dynamics (Pajares, 2006).

With the Board focusing on progressive changes to the Community Cooperative, there appears to be alignment with Bandura (2005) and the belief that self-efficacy is highly influential in ushering in change and progressive policies. With a goal of developing programming and assessments that will incentivize for-profit investment, the Board needs to believe that they possess the skills to accomplish the goal. This will require input from others in the field who have attempted to implement these types of changes. Successfully achieving this goal will also require observing others who have attempted this goal.

The self-efficacy of the Board is a predictor of the organizational commitment of the employees of an organization (Akhtar, Ghayas, & Adil, 2013). While self-efficacy might be one of the most important entrepreneurial traits for for-profit executives, it is also a fundamental requirement of an effective Board for a non-profit company (Lukes and Stephan, 2012). A Board's ability to practice self-efficacy directly influences the proficiency of their organization and the organization's ability to successfully complete an initiative (Brown & Fields 2011).

Table 3 shows the organizational performance goal and stakeholder goal that are critical to meeting the organizational and stakeholder goals. Further, the table identifies the motivational theory and the assessment mechanism suggested for the stakeholders.

Table 3

Motivational Influences and Motivational Influence Assessments

Assumed Motivation Influences	Motivational Influence Assessment
Value- The Board of Directors need to value private investment into non-profit initiatives.	This motivational influence will be assessed by interviews. Interviews will be conducted with stakeholders to determine whether stakeholders' values are in alignment with the organization's values. During the interview, stakeholders will be asked about the value they place on private investment compared to donations and other forms of income for the organization.
Self-Efficacy Theory- The Board of Directors must believe they can meet the performance goal of developing three programs that incentivize private investment through the relevant tasks that are required to reach this performance goals.	This motivational influence will be assessed by interviews. In the interview, stakeholders will be asked about whether they believe they can achieve the development and programming goals required to meet the organizational goal.

Organization- Related Influences

The third and final factor in an organization's success is the organizational influence that an organization has on its own performance gaps. This final component of the Clark and Estes (2008) knowledge, motivation, and organizational equation for analyzing and problem solving the gap between goals and performance, provides comprehensive answers to the disconnect that often occurs between different stakeholder groups. Organizations contribute to the deficiency and the proficiency of the skills and performance of the stakeholder groups tasked with closing performance gaps. Organizations that fail to support their stakeholder groups with adequate resources, processes, and culture are organizations that create performance gaps (Clark & Estes, 2008). In the next section, organization change will be analyzed, through the literature, according to cultural models and cultural settings in an effort to understand what influences will adequately support the Board of Directors of the Community Cooperative in achieving their goal.

The style of leadership and the policies that inform organizational character and practices are born out of an organization's culture. Organizational culture is defined as the values, goals, beliefs, and processes within an organization that develop as the organization scales and dictates how employees complete tasks (Clark & Estes, 2008). Culture connects the different people in an organization so that they share common goals in a manner that allows the organization to accomplish desired outcomes (Bolman & Deal, 2013). In this way, culture operates as a product of work experience and a process of organizational development (Bolman & Deal, 2013).

Cultural Settings and Models

Organizational culture is comprised of cultural models and settings (Gallimore & Goldenberg, 2001). Cultural models are institutional practices and shared understandings within an organization (Gallimore & Goldenberg, 2001). Cultural settings are the manifestation of the cultural model and is best exemplified by how members of the organization work together to complete tasks (Gallimore & Goldenberg, 2001). Cultural settings are typically fixed, concrete, and include the social context in which work is completed (Gallimore & Goldenberg, 2001). The visible characteristics of an organization and the underlying assumptions about the organization is an accurate description of an organization's cultural settings and models (Schein, 2004).

By studying cultural models and settings, the research will identify and examine organizational influences such as trust, accountability, goal setting and communication. In order to achieve the organizational goal of incentivizing private investment in the Community Cooperative's non-profit initiatives, the Board will be required to hold each other accountable, clearly communicate the goals and status of each required task and provide the resources necessary for accomplishing organizational goals.

Accountability

The Board of The Community Cooperative must hold each other accountable for the development of programming that achieves the organizational goal of private investment. Firestone and Riehl (2005) defined accountability as the requirement to account for performance to another by explanation of method and reporting of outcomes. In this current study, the Board of the Community Cooperative must be honest with one another in explaining their respective methods for data collection and honestly report the outcomes of their collections. These collections will inform their programming and provide the data required to show patterns of success in impact investment programs. Without a focus on accountability, organizations typically have low performance rates and a misunderstanding of the granular activities of an organization (Kezar, 2001). Bolman and Deal (2010) assert that high performing teams have a system of automatic individual and team accountability.

With a focus on accountability as a cultural setting, the Community Cooperative can foster a culture of accountability and exhibit work patterns of accountability (Clark & Estes, 2008). This would enable the Community Cooperative to quickly identify and exclude bad data or programming and streamline finding effective methods of incentivizing private investment. This streamlined approach would also allow the Community Cooperative to deliver efficient services and effectively manage the corresponding costs.

Clearly Communicate Goals

Goal setting is a cultural setting that provides an organization with purpose and vision (Hess & Bacigalupo, 2013). Goal setting also provides an organization with validity as the organization works internally uniformly in accomplishing goals (Hess & Bacigalupo, 2013). Since individual employee goals are based on organizational goals, organizational goals remain the standard of organizational progress (Lewis, 2011). By sharing goals and fostering organizational consensus, employees are able to focus on organizational goals and spend less time on individual focus (Clark & Estes, 2008). When organizational goals are clearly identified, employees can typically rely on a pattern of conduct to accomplish goals within the organization. This is true for the Community Cooperative because as participants and instructors develop as vested members of the Community Cooperative community, these same participants and instructors place an increased value on organizational goals and the tasks required to achieve them.

Effective communication is key to effective goal setting. The use of common language is essential to goal-setting and accountability (Krathwohl, 2002). A lack of communication can break a relationship down and lead to lack of trust and disenfranchisement (Blery, Katseli & Tsara, 2010). Alternatively, good communication develops trust and employee engagement, a lack of clear vision can also break down the willingness of supporters to support a work (Blery, et al, 2010). Blery, Katseli and Tsara (2010) also posit that when an organization clearly states its goals and provides a roadmap for its work, the employees can focus on processing desired outcomes. With a focus on communication and transparency, the Community Cooperative will provide a clear path toward proficiency for members, participants and instructors.

Provide the Necessary Resources

While accountability and clear communication inform organizational proficiency, providing the necessary resources for accomplishing organizational goals is also evidence of a cultural setting required for the Community Cooperative to achieve its organizational goals. This commitment to resources designed to better capture and understand data will be required in order for the Community Cooperative to scale in proficiency and private investment (Schein, 2017). To this end, the Community Cooperative will provide the required resources to capture and analyze data that will incentivize private investment. This data includes participant assessments, participant retention and the relationship between funding and programming.

In order to effectively explain the importance of programming for the Community Cooperative, this section discussed the K, M and O influences. The knowledge and motivation influences provide a lens into the individual stakeholders of the Community Cooperative. The organizational influences are illustrated in Table 4.

Table 4

Organizational Influences

Assumed Organizational Influences	Organizational Influence Assessment
Cultural Setting - The Community Cooperative needs a structure of accountability with private investment related to program performance and data collection.	Interviews to assess the accountability of the Community Cooperative. Document Analysis to determine the viability of the assessment process.
Cultural Setting - The Community Cooperative needs clearly defined program goals that are communicated to potential investors.	Interviews to assess the level of communication within the Community Cooperative.
Cultural Setting – The Community Cooperative needs resources devoted to the development of data that will incentivize private investment.	Interviews and document analysis of presently and publicly available documents to assess the current resources being allocated to the development of data.

Conceptual Framework: The Interaction of Stakeholders' Knowledge and Motivation and The Organizational Context

Understanding the process of incentivizing private investment in non-profit initiatives for the purpose of this study requires a conceptual framework. A conceptual framework gives direction and focus to a study by identifying general themes related to the topic of the study (Maxwell, 2013). Merriam and Tisdell (2016) assert that the theoretical framework affects each aggregate part contained within a body of research, including key terms, concepts, literature, and undeveloped studies that may affect the focus of research. In the current study, the conceptual framework (Figure 2) focuses on what the Board of Directors of the Community Cooperative will be required to learn and execute in order to incentivize private investment. The next section will discuss how the knowledge, motivation, and organizational factors introduced above intersect to form the foundation of the conceptual framework and exemplify the framework through a graphical depiction (Figure 1).

The Community Cooperative's Board of Directors have K and M factors that directly contribute to their ability to incentivize private investors to invest in non-profit initiatives of the organization. The K and M influences of each individual Board Member are influenced and directly affected by the influences of the organization. To this point, the Board of the Community Cooperative must know the importance of private investment and how to proficiently develop programming. Additionally, Board Members need to believe that they can meet the goal as a symbol of self-efficacy (Bongar, et al. 2017). This conceptual framework posits that these knowledge and motivation influences coupled with organizational cultural models, settings and resources will ensure success. Thus, the knowledge, motivation, and organization factors within the organization are most effective when interaction between all three occurs, as represented in

Figure 1.

Figure 1

Conceptual Framework for the Community Cooperative

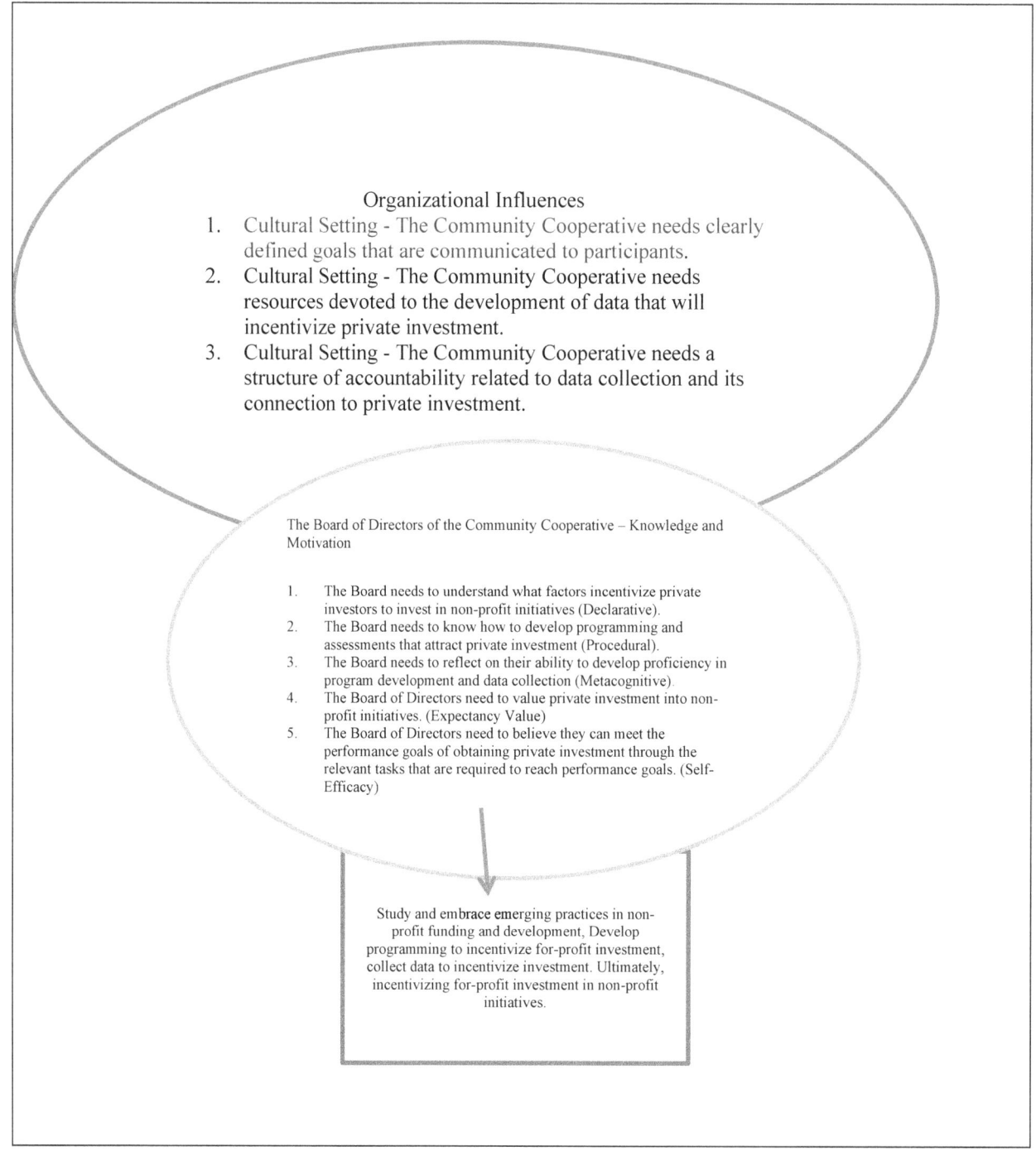

The figure further represents how the knowledge, motivation, and organizational influences factor within the two and the collective work that they both require:

1. The orange ring is representative of the stakeholder group identified as the Board of the Community Cooperative and the organizational factors.

2. The blue ring is representative of the organization. Cultural settings indicative of the organization are present within this circle.

3. The work required to achieve the stakeholder and the organizational goal is represented by the purple square. While the goal is ultimately incentivizing for-profit investment, embracing the process and skills required to meet this goal is itself a goal.

The Board Members of the Community Cooperative must be proficient in specific knowledge and motivation factors in order to meet their goals. Procedural knowledge of programming that will incentivize private investment is crucial. Declarative and conceptual knowledge of the importance of private investment must be present in order to inspire the Board to remain consistent in its efforts. Self-efficacy is also a key factor to the success of the Board as this motivational factor allows the Board to believe that the knowledge and organizational factors available can allow them to succeed in procuring private investment. While the knowledge and motivation factors described above are important as independent factors, in this conceptual framework the knowledge and motivation factors are interdependent upon the Community Cooperative as an organization to which the Board are also participant members.

The Community Cooperative is the organization that holds the Board Members accountable. However, the Community Cooperative as an organization contains critical organizational factors such as cultural settings, cultural models, resources and processes. Cultural settings and models are represented in the blue circle of the framework. The conceptual framework assumes these cultural settings and models are necessary for achieving the organizational goal, but they depend upon the Board being proficient in their respective knowledge and motivation factors to succeed.

With the three knowledge, motivation and organizational factors and influencers being interdependent for the achievement of the organizational goal, each part of the organization relies on each other. Without the stakeholders and their knowledge and motivation influences and factors, the organization lacks a programming that provides data that incentivizes private investment. Without the organization, the Board ceases to exist and the individuals on the Board are left with no cultural setting. Thus, the conceptual framework asserts that all knowledge, motivation and organizational factors, as well as the relationship between the Community Cooperative and its Board, are necessary for success in incentivizing private investment in non-profit initiatives.

Summary

The purpose of this study is to evaluate how non-profit organizations might incentivize for-profit investment. This literature review included research in the differing desired outcomes of non-profit and for-profit companies and some effective examples of creating intersection between their differing value systems. The literature in chapter two provided examples of public private partnerships and distinguished between socially responsible investing and impact investing. The literature also identified that impact investing creates better synergy between non-profit and for profit entities because impact investing is an investment that ties return on investment directly to social good. This study also identified the knowledge, motivation, and organizational influences of the Board of Directors for the Community Cooperative and provided the conceptual framework for the problem of practice. In the next section, chapter three, the research will present the study's methodological approach.

CHAPTER THREE: METHODS

This chapter represents the study's research and design methods for the collection of data and the analysis of subject data. In evaluating the Community Cooperative's Board of Directors' knowledge, motivation and organizational influences related to achieving the organizational goal of incentivizing private investment in their non-profit initiatives, this study was guided by several questions. The questions that guided this study were:

1. What are the Board of Director's knowledge and motivation related to incentivizing private investment in non-profit initiatives?

2. What is the interaction between organizational culture and context and the Board of Directors' knowledge and motivation to increase private investment in non-profit initiatives?

3. What are the recommendations for organizational practice in the areas of knowledge, motivation and organizational resources related to private investment into non-profit initiatives?

The sampling criteria, recruitment strategy, and rationale for the data collection method is also identified in this chapter. Additionally, the chapter provides additional reasoning behind the data collection methods and analysis.

Participating Stakeholders

While the success of an organization is never determined by one stakeholder group, the leadership of an organization is often an effective indicator of the direction of an organization and their potential for success. As the policy makers in an organization, the Board of Directors create the framework for how an organization works. The Community Cooperative operates in a very unique way as the Board of Directors not only create policy for the organization, the Board

Members also manages the day to day leadership of the organization. As the policy makers and executors, the Board of the Community Cooperative have the deepest understanding of the organization's work, the field in which they work, and the greatest potential for providing relevant data to this study. These factors clearly indicate why the Board of the Community Cooperative are the stakeholders of focus for this study.

Individual Interview Sampling Criterion and Rationale

As the researcher was excluded from the study, all eight of the additional Board Members of the Community Cooperative participated in this study. The Board Members have a specific lens into the creation of organizational policy and its execution. Additionally, the Board is uniquely placed in leadership to observe how policies are effective or ineffective. Board Members have established a commitment to the non-profit initiatives of the organization and have actively participated in the work of the organization. This experience and commitment provide the requisite knowledge of the Board member and establishes the requisite motivation of the Board Member. All Board Members of the Community Cooperative have given at least ten thousand dollars in currency or resources to the organization. This financial commitment establishes the understanding of the financial needs of the Community Cooperative and also establishes the Board Members' understanding of the need for private investment in the Community Cooperative.

Interview Sampling Strategy and Rationale

For the interviews of the stakeholder group of focus, the sampling was a census sample (Creswell, 2014; Fink, 2013; Merriam & Tisdell, 2016). The census sampling of participants was designed to create a group that would possess the requisite knowledge of the field and organization, from which meaningful qualitative discovery will be conducted (Merriam & Tisdell, 2016). Additionally, the conduct and activities of the entire Board was studied. With all eight additional members of the Board being interviewed, a realistic sample size was delivered. Limiting the size of the study also rendered the study stratified, with participants reflecting conduct that can be accurately attributed to the whole group (Creswell, 2016). For this study, stratification means including Board Members who are founding members and Board Members who have joined in not less than three years. Recruitment for this study was relatively easy as the focus group had spent a great amount of time looking for methods to improve private investment. A study of the organization's knowledge, motivation and organizational influences required to solve this problem of practice is recognized as a good thing internally and all Board Members have already offered to participate.

Explanation of Choices

The Board of Directors of the Community Cooperative represented the stakeholder group with the most information to offer for this study. For that reason alone, the study focused on the Board of Directors. The qualitative method is the most effective method to use when analyzing research that is driven by narrative. The interview method also appears to provide the most qualitative information as surveys only provide a snapshot of the process of decision-making.

Using the interview method and the census method to triangulate data gathered from the other methods for the purpose of revealing research themes (Creswell, 2014), reduces bias and incidental intersections of information (Maxwell, 2013) and increases validity and credibility (Merriam & Tisdell, 2016). This evaluation did not use surveys as the qualitative interviews and document analysis provided the most comprehensive information for this study.

Documents and Artifacts

The study collected documents from the Community Cooperative that aid in understanding how the Community Cooperative collects data that can be shared with potential investors. These documents included participant assessments from coding exercises and accountings separated by donations, fees for services and investments. These documents were publicly available and no participant, personal or pedigree data was revealed. These documents were voluntarily offered to the researcher by the Community Cooperative. An analysis of these documents provided additional context into how the results of non-profit work have a direct impact on the funding of non-profit work. Focusing on participant experiences and growth provided broader context into the effectiveness of the organization and its ability to scale in funding (Creswell, 2014; Merriam & Tisdell, 2016).

Comparing participant interview responses with available data allowed the researcher to get accurate responses to questions that might be affected by the participants' biases. While participants provided responses that were optimistic about the Community Cooperatives' conceptual knowledge and values related to incentivizing private investment, the interviews and publicly available data helped temper responses that may have been based on intent and not impact. Specifically, the interviews and available documentation helped the researcher understand what accountability methods are currently not in place and what missing resources are needed to develop and analyze data that will incentivize private investment.

Qualitative Data Collection

Creswell (2014) asserts that qualitative research requires the collection of multiple forms of data. These different methods of data collection allow for broader contextual understanding of the knowledge, motivation and organization influences associated with participant responses (Creswell, 2014; Merriam & Tisdell, 2016). This study included two types of qualitative data: interviews and document analysis. The researcher conducted interviews with Board Members of the Community Cooperative to document their knowledge, motivation and experience related to their organizational goal of incentivizing private investment in the organizations' initiatives.

Interviews

Eight interviews were conducted with the other Board Members of the Community Cooperative. These interviews ranged from 40 minutes to one hour, with most interviews lasting one hour. All participants being interviewed volunteered for this study and were not pressured to participate in this study. The researcher administered the interviews in a formal manner in an effort to maintain a consistent process in the data collection process and to limit any bias that might have affected the integrity of the process (Merriam & Tisdell, 2016). The interview subjects were given optional times over the course of one month in an effort to accommodate their busy schedules and make the process as easy as possible. Remaining amenable to their schedules is important to maintaining their willingness to engage in the process. The interview questions were straight-forward and open-ended in order to elicit the most thoughtful and complete responses (Patton, 2002). The interview protocol elicited meaningful data from the Board of the Community Collective related to their organizational experiences and knowledge and motivation (see Appendix A).

Documents and Artifacts

The study collected documents from the Community Cooperative that aided in understanding how the Community Cooperative collects data that can be shared with potential investors (see Appendix B). These documents included participant assessments from coding exercises and accountings separated by donations, fees for services and investments. These documents were publicly available and no participant personal or background data was revealed. These documents were voluntarily offered to the researcher by the Community Cooperative. An analysis of these documents provided additional context into how the results of non-profit work have a direct impact on the funding. Focusing on participant experiences and financial growth provided broader context into the effectiveness of the organization and its ability to scale in funding (Creswell, 2014; Merriam & Tisdell, 2016).

Comparing participant interview responses with available data allowed the researcher to triangulate responses to questions that might have affected by the participants' biases. While participants provided responses that were optimistic about the Community Cooperatives' conceptual knowledge and values related to incentivizing private investment, the interviews and publicly available data helped temper responses that were based on intent instead of impact. Specifically, the interviews and available documentation helped the researcher understand what accountability methods were currently in place and what resources were being used to develop and analyze data that incentivize private investment.

Data Analysis

In order to obtain comprehensive data from this study, the researcher conducted interviews and document reviews. Interviewing allows the participant to share information that is centered on their own experiences and perceptions and provided the interviewer with the best opportunity to contextualize the participant's responses (Merriam & Tisdell, 2016). The interviews and document review began during data collection. The researcher wrote memos and notes during and after each interview. All questions, concerns or comments were noted by the researcher and compared to the conceptual framework and research questions. Once the interviews were complete, the researcher coded and transcribed the interviews. Coding allowed the researcher to use short-hand notes that were easy to refer to once the researcher compared the responses to research questions to the conceptual framework (Merriam & Tisdell, 2016). Once the coding was complete, the researcher analyzed documents and artifacts in relation to the concepts in the conceptual framework.

The researcher used open coding during the analysis of the interviews and document review. Comparing the questions and responses to a priori codes from the conceptual framework allowed the researcher to categorize responses according to prompts in the conceptual framework. The researcher then used these response codes to create analytical codes that the researcher used to identify patterns of thought, conduct and beliefs. These patterns of thought, conduct and beliefs were then analyzed within the conceptual framework and used to analyze knowledge, motivation and organizational influences and gaps.

Credibility and Trustworthiness

As the main instrument in a qualitative study, the researcher is tasked with using methods that ensure the research is credible and trustworthy (Creswell, 2014). This required the appropriate effort and attention to ethical conduct throughout all of the research and a commitment to the process of being accountable to the highest ethical standards (Merriam & Tisdell, 2016). In an effort to ensure the validity of the research, the researcher also reviewed publicly available documents in order to compare findings. This collection and comparison of findings was a method of triangulation to ensure internal validity (Creswell, 2014; Merriam & Tisdell, 2016). By using interview questions that draw out deep context, meaning and thought from the participants, the data provided was rich in substance.

Engaging in reflexivity allowed the researcher to reflect on biases, roles in the organization and assumptions that might affect data so that the credibility and trustworthiness of the data was not tainted (Creswell, 2014; Merriam & Tisdell, 2016). Journaling the process and reflecting on my bias and how it affects my process benefitted the study and the results were more accurate and impactful (Creswell, 2014; Merriam & Tisdell, 2016).

Ethics

Ethical practice and informed consent were foundational to the research provided in this study. All inquiry, data and development were scaffolded with ethical considerations (Glesne, 2011). These ethical considerations included a focus on doing no harm, avoiding deception or pressure on participants, obtaining informed consent, and honoring the promises and expectations of the participants (Rubin & Rubin, 2012; Tracy, 2013). In this study, participants were not placed in any position of risk because the interview questions did not probe into confidential or sensitive subjects. The purpose of this study was clearly communicated to participants by the principal researcher in preliminary conversations related to this study and then reiterated in writing to participants through the dissemination of an information sheet. The information sheet provided to the participants with information was suggested by Glesne (2011), and included the participants' right to decline or withdraw participation at anytime and the potential risks of participating. Additionally, the Board of Directors of the Community Cooperative unanimously voted to participate in this study.

Participants in this study maintained an expectation of privacy that was protected (Glesne, 2011). To this end, no identifiable information was collected or obtained and participants were not asked to reveal their identities. All interview notes were kept in a secure location where only the principal researcher had access to the data and the notes were destroyed when the study was concluded.

One of the most important tasks required to deliver rich and reliable data is to identify bias and provide transparency. Thus, it is must be noted that the principal researcher is a Board Member of the Community Cooperative and a major stakeholder in the organization. This status within the organization informed the principal researcher's decision to only interview other

Board Members so that no subordinates would be subject to the potential biases or pressures associated with participating in this study. By interviewing peer-level colleagues, the principal researcher can cull information from members of the organization who are vested in the success of the study and thus very interested in providing data that is free from bias (Creswell, 2014). And while the researcher and the participants share an interest in a well-executed study, no researcher or participant had any specific material stake in the study or personally benefit from its findings.

The researcher chose not to have an outside interviewer conduct the interviews because the participants in the study are all aware of the researcher's identity and purpose. The best way to demonstrate respect for the study and eliminate any power imbalances is to engage them in an honest and transparent manner (Creswell, 2014). Additionally, since the Community Cooperative operates in a cyclical structure with no formal hierarchy, the researcher has no influencing power or authority over the participants being interviewed and did not create involuntary participation or uninformed consent (Glesne, 2011).

Because the researcher is the primary instrument for data collection, the personal biases of the researcher must be noted (Merriam & Tisdell, 2016). The researcher is a firm believer that capitalism has caused a vacuum in human values that is driving the human path toward unsustainability. While the researcher shares many of the values of socialism (means of production and consumption controlled by the people), the researcher understands the practical need for capital and governance in partnership in order for societal shifts to be realized. While the researcher's personal views should be noted in light of this study on private investment in non-profit initiatives, these views did not negatively bias the data gathered related to the other stakeholders. Additionally, the data collection process was triangulated through interviews and historical documents in an effort to limit the effect of researcher bias on the study (Merriam &

Tisdell, 2016; Tracey, 2013).

CHAPTER FOUR: FINDINGS

Chapter Four is the presentation of the findings of this study through an analysis of the knowledge, motivation and organizational influences as informed by the Clark and Estes' (2008) gap analysis framework. Each of the knowledge, motivation and organization influences introduced in Chapter Two are analyzed through the findings. A comprehensive analysis of each assumed influence will also be provided in addition to whether a gap was identified for the assumed influence. Interviews and document data were collected to analyze the knowledge, motivation and organizational proficiencies and deficiencies that might affect the Community Cooperative's ability to incentivize private investment in its non-profit initiatives.

Research Questions

The research questions that guided this study were:

1. What are the Board of Director's knowledge and motivation related to incentivizing private investment in non-profit initiatives?

2. What is the interaction between organizational culture and context and Board of Directors' knowledge and motivation to increase private investment in non-profit initiatives?

3. What are the recommendations for organizational practice in the areas of knowledge, motivation and organizational resources related to private investment into non-profit initiatives? Using a qualitative analysis of these interviews and documents, the researcher has provided answers to the research questions being raised.

Participants

Eight members of the Board of Directors of the Community Cooperative were interviewed for this study. To protect the identity of individual participants, no demographic or other identifying information is provided. Each participant was issued a number between 1 and 8 and identified as Participant 1-8 (P1-P8 in tables) for the purpose of this study.

Knowledge, Motivation, and Organizational Findings

The interviews were conducted as part of a qualitative analysis. Text message requests to participate in the study and be interviewed were sent by the researcher to each board member. Each board member responded in the affirmative within one day of the initial text. For each interview, 23 questions were asked with no follow up or additional questions or remarks from the researcher. The interviews were conducted over zoom and recorded. Each subject gave explicit permission to be interviewed and to have the interviews recorded and transcribed. Each interview was transcribed by Otter.ai. All interviews lasted less than an hour. The responses to the interview questions have been placed in a secure location and have not been shared with anyone. The responses were then analyzed for the qualitative findings of this study.

Knowledge Findings

This study's knowledge research question is: What are the board of director's knowledge related to incentivizing private investment in non-profit initiatives? The answer to this question is found in comparing the interviewees' responses to the conceptual, procedural and metacognitive knowledge influences proposed in Chapter Two. Additionally, the document review revealed that the board was consistent in reflecting on their ability to develop programming and data collection that furthered the organizational goal. While the board's conceptual and metacognitive knowledge influences did not appear to reveal any gaps, the board did appear to need improvement in procedural knowledge. This was exemplified by the board's inability to articulate the process for implementing and programming and data collection. Implementing data collection and programming are key components required to incentivize private investment. This section presents a summary of the findings from the interviews and document analysis separately before addressing

key themes that were identified through the course of the study.

Interviews

The researcher conducted interviews as part of a qualitative approach. The interview

questions were structured so that the responses would reveal how the knowledge influences

impacted the Board Members' proficiency in developing programming and data that would

incentivize private investment. The questions were consistent with the conceptual framework and

included the following:

1. Describe how private investors determine which non-profit initiatives

   to invest in, if any.

2. What are some metrics private investors look for when deciding what to

   invest in?

3. What are some desired outcomes for private investors when deciding

   what to invest in?

4. What programs, if any, do investors look for when deciding what to

   invest in?

5. What have you observed about the process of collecting data that

   informs private investment?

All eight Board Members were assigned numbers from one through eight and asked the

above questions during the interview process. The participants all responded to questions related

to their conceptual knowledge in a manner that indicated a basic understanding of what factors

incentivize private investors to invest in non-profit initiatives. The participants also responded to

questions related to their metacognitive knowledge in a manner that indicated their assessment and reflection on their ability to develop proficiency in program development and data collection that incentivizes private investment. However, a procedural knowledge gap occurred as the participants struggled to describe how to develop programming and assessments that attract private investment. A sample of the knowledge influences interview results are represented by Table 5 following a narrative discussion of the findings.

As illustrated in Table 5, the interviews with the Board Members included questions related to the influences that might be considered conceptual, procedural and metacognitive. There did not appear to be a conceptual knowledge gap as the participants were generally able to articulate what factors incentivize private investors to invest in non-profit initiatives. The participants also appeared to thoroughly reflect on their ability to develop proficiency in program development and data collection. By thoroughly reflecting on their ability to stay on task with the organizational goals, the participants did not appear to show a metacognitive knowledge gap.

However, when the participants were asked questions related to the process or implementation of programming and data collection that would incentivize private investment, their responses were vague, general, or non-responsive. For example, when asked about the implementation of programming, Participant 1stated, "programming is developed based on need and resources" while Participant 3 responded, "I don't have any experience there." These responses revealed a lack of the procedural knowledge required to implement the data collection and programming required to incentivize private investment. The questions that were designed to explore procedural knowledge gaps should have prompted responses that identified some specific program opportunities, parallel outcomes, and metrics for success that the participants could call out as a model for implementation. However, there appeared to be a lack of confidence and training in implementation models that currently work to incentivize private investment in non-profits.

While most participants attempted to provide an adequate response, when Participant 8 was asked to describe the metrics private investors look for when investing in nonprofits, this board member transparently replied, "I don't know." Based on the replies to the questions in this section, there appears to be a procedural knowledge gap in the goal to develop programming and data collection that would incentivize private investment.

Table 5

Knowledge Influences, Interview Results

Knowledge Influences, Interview Results		
Interview Questions	Knowledge Type	Responses
Describe how private investors determine which non-profit initiatives to invest in, if any?	Conceptual	P1- "a smart investor would …see how a program works and how you're getting resources…" P4- "the investors' perception of how the world views the non-profit" P7- "a lifestyle choice…the non-profit aligns with [the investor's values]"
What are some metrics private investors look for when deciding what to invest in?	Procedural	P2- "Credit worthiness, if that's a word if that makes sense" P3- "Yeah I don't have an answer for that one" P5- "Just human interaction" P6- "the ability to maintain the status quo or social control." P8- "I don't know"

What are some desired outcomes for private investors when deciding what to invest in?	Procedural	P2- "I guess it depends on who you're investing in, like, if you invest in a community outreach nonprofit, I would hope that you…change crime drops, they're reaching the kids and education is improving." P3- "return on their money…to see whatever they're investing in blossom." P4- "as in any relationship they want to see an observable return"
What programs, if any, do investors look for when deciding what to invest in?	Procedural	P1- Programs "that are near and dear to their heart." P5- "In my experience, things that have to do with people who are formerly incarcerated has been a major one along with environmental awareness being another one." P7- "Environment, Education and Technology"
What have you observed about the process of collecting data that informs private investment?	Metacognitive	P1- "That is critical because when we do a particular program, we did an eight week program and in Red Hook with kids in middle school, and the data is key to help tell the story and to help communicate your findings with you know, set investor, anyone really a potential parent who may want their kid to be part of your curriculum, we like, you know, the data is it helps a lot It also helps as a marker of success. So you can base you know, how successful was our program, how, how

successful Can this be if we add the certain elements or remove these certain elements, so data is very useful. Very important."

P6- "I think one of the things that I'm most proud of ... is that we really, in my opinion, we've been focusing on the interaction with humanity and the people. I'm not. And I think that's one of our, I think, depending on who you speak to a lot of people may come away with the fact that they feel we should be reaching out more to investors and getting investments and grants. But I think we've kind of been really enthralled in how can we impact on the ground? So I am and I know me for one, I'm much more interested in that maybe there's others in our organization or other people who can focus on getting the the invest investment side of it, but I'm not particularly smitten by that, to be honest with you."

Document Review

The document review examined student attendance and proficiency rates in coding exercises from 2018 through 2019 as well as donations and investments. The data from the document review revealed that there were no investments, very few donations from people outside of the Board and that the participants in this study have placed an emphasis on reflecting on their ability to develop proficiency in program development and data collection. This metacognitive knowledge will be important for the participants as they continue to develop programming and collect data that is in alignment with the organization's goals. Attendance was taken and proficiency assessments were documented for 100% of the mentoring programs provided by the Community Cooperative. The document review also examined the completion rate of assessments in order to determine if program development goals could be informed by student participation.

The document review examined three programs developed and run by the Community Cooperative. The programs are partnerships with local communities in Brownsville, Red Hook and East New York. The partners are host sites that have students in the community that either volunteer to attend programming or are mandated by their school or other governing authority. While 100% of the students involved in the CREAM Center (pseudonym) partnership completed the creation of their Bluetooth speakers, 85% of the students at the Scott Hill (pseudonym) partnership completed creation of their websites, and 100% of the students at the SUMMISE school (pseudonym) partnership completed creation of their websites. This success rate indicates that the programming is being created effectively and in a manner that keeps learners engaged.

Knowledge Theme 1: Board Members Understand What Incentivizes Private Investors

By analyzing the interviews and documents, the Board Members understand what factors incentivize private investors to invest in non-profit initiatives. When posed with guiding questions related to private investment in non-profit initiatives, Participant 1 in the study provided insightful information. Participant 1 stated:

Somehow connecting with the nonprofit that they're investing in, and getting a look at how they do their practice, how they, you know, in our case, you know, we work with the community. So, in some instances, you know, you would invite the investor down and they would sit with you and see kind of How your program works, you know, what is involved?

Who is affected? Who's being helped, and how you're getting them the resources.

This shows the participant's the knowledge related to incentivizing private investment in non-profit initiatives. The participant is clear on the importance of private investment. This knowledge of the importance of the organizational goal provides a foundation for developing the programming necessary to incentivize private investment. Participant 4 remarked, "it would be similar to commercial ventures in that they (private investors) would want to see a direct relationship between the investment, good work and a good return." This sentiment is generally shared among the other participants, including Participant 6, who stated, " [if an investor] does not understand a non-profit or the non-profit's goal and how it's connected to the investor, that may have an impact on their willingness to invest." The data makes it clear that the participants had a strong conceptual knowledge of the problem of practice presented in the study.

Knowledge Theme 2: Board Members are Reflective of Their Ability to Collect Data and Create Programming

The data reveals that the participants reflected on their ability to develop proficiency in program development and data collection. Each of the participants provided thoughtful and well-informed reflections about their ability to develop programming and data collection that incentivized private investment. When asked to describe areas in which they would seek growth in their ability to explain programs in a manner that would attract private investors, Participant 3 responded:

We could use tools like some of the events where we actually have the people who we work with as well as the people who we've worked for speak and give some accounts of how the Cooperative has changed their lives and how they have gone into the community to pay it forward. Having community members speak for themselves would be far more impactful because they are the product of these partnerships we are seeking.

When posed with the same prompt, participant 8 responded:

"I would want to collect data better and track kids that have gone through the program and it really matters their growth. Um, and not just from a, like, logical standpoint of like, Oh, they can now build a program but also like emotional growth, things like that if we've raised the quality of life I've seen I see examples, we just don't have those case studies to document it. So, I think that's where I would like to take home our product and refine it and present it, like constantly present it."

The responses from Participant 3 and Participant 8 are indicative of the thoughtful and insightful responses from all of the participants when prompted with questions related to their metacognitive knowledge influence on the problem of practice.

Knowledge Theme 3: The Board of Directors Need to Know how to Develop Programming and Assessments that Attract Private Investment

While the participants understand the importance of private investment in non-profit initiatives and are deeply reflective of the work required to achieve the stakeholder and organizational goal, all of the participants lacked complete proficiency in the process of developing programming and assessments that attract private investment. When asked, what programs, if any, do investors look for when deciding what to invest in, Participant 3 responded, "I have no answer for that one." When prompted with the same question, Participant 5 stated, "it's a struggle." All of the participants answered these questions similarly. This "struggle" indicates that the participants have a knowledge gap as it relates to their ability to create and implement programming that will yield data that incentivizes private investment. The gap between knowing the importance of a practice and knowing how to implement a practice is the challenge facing the Community Cooperative. The participants are all skilled at reflecting and acknowledging these challenges. This metacognitive knowledge will be a helpful tool as the stakeholders develop proficiency in procedural knowledge.

Motivation Findings

This study's motivation research question is: What is the Board of Director's motivation related to incentivizing private investment in non-profit initiatives? The data gathered during interviews reveals that the Board is highly motivated to engage in the work of incentivizing private investment but has a motivation gap in the area of self-efficacy. This section presents a summary of the findings from interviews and document analysis before proceeding into a discussion of the key themes that emerged from the qualitative analysis.

Interviews

The researcher divided the interview questions into the two motivational theories of expectancy-value and self-efficacy. The motivation research asked questions about the Board of Directors' motivation related to incentivizing private investment in non-profit initiatives. The relevant interview questions and responses are described in Table 6 following the narrative discussion of the findings.

The general sentiment shared among participants was that private investment in the organization's work was important. The participants placed a great deal of value on obtaining private investment and communicated high levels of motivation to seek ways to implement private partnerships into the work of the organization. Participant 1 acknowledged that the needs of non-profits exceed the donation amounts and that there is an increasing need for partnerships that yield returns tied to social good. Participant 5 acknowledged that in order for the organization to be sustainable, private investment was necessary.

While the participants did recognize the value of private investment, some also acknowledged the inherent dangers that can occur in partnerships where values may not be aligned. While Participant 2 stated, "I can't imagine there being any detriments in non-profits receiving funding," Participant 8 asserts, "but the investor can't feel like they own you." This commitment to core organizational values provides a balancing act for the participants as they seek to invite private investment that is in alignment with their values.

Similarly, to the procedural knowledge gap, the participants appeared to waiver in confidence when questioned about their abilities to create programming and collect data that might incentivize private investment. Participant 6 was most pointed in this regard when they stated:

> I've kind of limited myself, and I think in a lot of regards, because I didn't want to get bogged down with the data so much…you can lose sight of what you're really trying to do and what the narrative is really about.

Participant 4 noted the financial limitations of doing the day-to-day work of the organization while also trying to create programming and data that would be attractive to private partners. While motivated to continue the work of the organization, participants struggled to find the motivation to collect certain data that furthered organizational goals.

Table 6

Motivation Influences, Interview Results

Motivation Influences, Interview Findings		
Interview Questions	Motivational Theory	Responses

Why is it important for non-profits initiatives to receive private investment?	Value	P1: "Because non-profits have needs that go beyond donations….and Non-profits can't function without money" P3: "…to take the burden off of the people who have invested time [because] it's hard to be present…as well as try to find funds to make things happen…" P5: "you need outside investment to keep the engine running"
Are there any detriments to non-profit initiatives receiving private investment?	Value	P2: "I can't imagine there being any detriments in non-profits receiving funding" P8: "Once a client gives you money they feel like they own you. But with an investment, they may want things skewed but the investor can't feel like they own you"
Describe your proficiency in programming and data collection.	Self-Efficacy	P4: "I hope that I am" P6: I think in programming, I'm pretty proficient in a sense that I understand what we're trying to do and in… the activation that's required. Outside of that, I've kind of limited myself, and I think in a lot of regards, because I didn't want to get bogged down with the data so much…you can lose sight of what you're really trying to do and what the narrative is really about. So I've been more on the end of conception and ideology… getting things done and activations. I haven't been that instrumental in the collection of data…."

Describe what limits your ability to develop programming and data that incentivizes private investment.	Self-Efficacy	P7: "I will say operations is definitely one of them…being able to manage operational budget, um, I think those are some things that I definitely [need to develop]" P4: "the biggest limit is financially not being able to afford to focus a dedicated amount of time to Developing programming right now, we are doing the work that we can, whenever we can, and however we can. And while that has sustained us over these years, it is certainly not efficient. And I would say then the biggest two of the biggest stumbling blocks of like any other organization is time and money, you know what I mean? And they seem to always have to be twisted up together like that, but they tend to be you know, they tend to be there any number of creative ways, I'm not gonna expand on it now, but suffice to say, time and money are big prohibiting factors to me personally being a being able to develop programming that, you know, can solve a lot of our very immediate needs and desires."

Document Review

The document review included a list of tax credits available to investors that would serve as an incentive for private-public partnerships. While these documents address what might motivate potential partners to invest in the organization, these documents provide no motivational impetus for stakeholders of a non-profit organization that is already tax-exempt.

Motivation Theme 1: Value

All eight members of the Board value partnerships with for profit investors that yield positive change. Specifically, Participant 3 expressed excitement when discussing private investment because it would allow the participants to focus on the work of social change and be relieved of the burden of seeking donations. This sentiment was shared by Participant 4 who acknowledged that the work of funding a non-profit can be detrimental to the actual work of creating social change. Even Participant 8, who expressed concern over financial partners dictating purpose, shared in the sentiment that a for-profit partner might provide a focus on efficiency that allows the organization to function better and do the work better.

Motivation Theme 2: Self-Efficacy

All members of the Board expressed a lack of confidence in their ability to collect data and programming that incentivize private investment. This is in contrast to their desire to collect data and create programming that accomplish their collective goal. This issue appears to be related to an issue with self-efficacy where the Board Members do not believe that they can initially be successful at something they have never done before. With no model for successful implementation of their goal, the participants all expressed doubts about their abilities. Participant 7 acknowledged that collecting data and creating programming that will attract private investment is an area of needed growth for the participants. Participant 1 also acknowledged that seeking private investment will require the participants to leave their comfort zones and engage in work that requires a new set of skills. This sentiment is shared among the participants as they all generally struggle with the concept of implementation of a new set of data collection and program development.

Organizational Influence Findings

The research question that probed for organization-related influences as they impact the stakeholder goal is: What is the interaction between organizational culture and context and the Board of Directors' knowledge and motivation to develop programming and collect data that will increase private investment in non-profit initiatives? This multi-layered question requires an examination of the participant's knowledge and motivation as it relates to private investment. This question also requires an examination of the cultural settings of the organization and how the participant's knowledge and motivation interact with the organization's cultural settings. While the organization has a clear mechanism and platform to communicate its goals, vision and mandates, the organization does not have clear mandates or a bonus structure implemented to incentivize private investment in its non-profit initiatives.

For the organization section, the research asked guiding questions related to the Community Cooperative's needs for clearly defined goals that are communicated to potential investors, resources devoted to the development of data that will incentivize private investment, and a structure of shared accountability with private investment related to program performance and data collection. The relevant questions and the corresponding responses are described in Table 7.

Table 7

Organizational Influences, Interview Results

Organizational Influences, Interview Results		
Interview Question	Cultural Model or Setting	Responses

How does your organization communicate its' goals to participants?	Setting	P3: "email, text and in our meetings" P6: "consistent messaging and conversations" P7: "events, social media, emails, texts and social gatherings" P8: "weekly meetings, zoom calls and events"
What organizational mandates exist to ensure that data is collected that incentivizes private investment?	Setting	P1: "I wouldn't say there are any mandates at the moment. Yeah, no like mandates, but I think that there should be some in place, just to make sure that by the end of every, you know, year or we create sort of benchmarks so that, you know, we can actually take information that's, you know, been used and proven and apply that to getting that information into our materials that we share with potential investors…" P2: "I don't think we have that set up" P4: "We don't have any." P5: "I am not sure."
What benefits or bonuses exist for participants who collect data that incentivizes private investment?	Setting	P1: "there are no incentives. Just the incentive of being a team player participating in a positive way." P2: "there are no benefits" P5: "I'm not sure" P6: "there is none. We're doing it because it has to get done" P7: "none that I know of" P8: "none. We do this for the will not for a bonus"

The organizational settings appear to provide more information about the KMO factors affecting the organization than any cultural models. The participants' responses were generally uniform when discussing the organizational factors affecting the organization's desired goal.

Document Analysis

The researcher collected documents related to the current data collection efforts of the organization including attendance records of participants and the tax benefits available to private investors. These documents did not yield any relevant data for this section of the study related to the organizational influences.

Organization Setting Theme 1: Clear Communication

According to the interviews, the organization clearly communicates its goals to participants. All eight of the Board Members of the organization agree that the organization's programmatic goals of mentoring and training that lead to community and workforce development are being communicated to potential investors through consistent attendance and assessments that exhibit the development of strong proficiencies in coding, conflict resolution and content creation. Through a partnership with STREAM, the Community Cooperative developed a content creation program where participants in the program created Bluetooth speakers and created marketing campaigns for household products. This program, the attendance, and its resulting marketing campaigns were sent to the organization's potential investors through a newsletter and follow up emails. It is worth noting that these perspectives were collected from the Board Members and not from volunteers. The researcher did not interview volunteers to determine if this theme was consistent with volunteers' perception.

Organization Setting Theme 2: Lack of Accountability for Data Collection

The organization does not appear to have mandates set up to ensure that participants collect data and create programming that incentivizes private investment. The participants were in unison on this issue. Participant 1, recognizing that there were no mandates in place, offered the suggestion that some mandates should be set in place in order to hold the stakeholder accountable for their responsibility in achieving the organizational goal. Participant 2 and Participant 5 did not definitively assert that there was no mandate, however, they both acknowledged not knowing of a mandate. Since the participants did not know of a mandate, it is clear that there is no mandate set up to ensure data is collected and programming is developed to further the organizational goal of incentivizing private investment in its non-profit initiatives.

Organization Theme 3: The Incentive Setting

According to the interviews with the participants, there are no incentives for collecting data that furthers the organizational goals. Participant 1 asserts that "just the incentive of being a team player" exists to incentivize participants. This statement is indicative of a larger theme among the participants in that they all appear to love the organization and its goals while also recognizing the lack of accountability necessary to meet the organization's goals. Participant 6 goes a step further and says that "there is none…we're doing it because it has to get done." This statement from Participant 6 reveals that the participants are aware of the organizational goal and the necessity to implement the strategies to accomplish the goal. Participant 8 states, "we do this for the will not for the bonus." The participants all expressed a loyalty and dedication to the organization and its goals. This loyalty and dedication to the organization indicates very motivated participants that have personal values in alignment with the organization's goal to grow in services and funding.

Synthesis

The results from this study reveal a group of stakeholders with conceptual knowledge of the importance of private investment in non-profit initiatives and the requisite metacognitive ability to reflect on the requirements to collect data and create programming that accomplish this goal. However, there was a gap in the stakeholder's procedural knowledge of how to implement the practices and strategies necessary to accomplish the organizational goals. As discussed in Chapter Three, a commitment to resources designed to better capture and understand data will be required in order for the Community Cooperative to scale in proficiency and private investment (Schein, 2017).

With detailed attendance and proficiency records, the document review revealed that the stakeholders take data collection seriously and already have a practice of monitoring attendance and proficiency in the mentoring programs that exist in three different sites. This supports the notion that the stakeholders are capable of developing the procedural knowledge necessary to develop programming that will incentivize private investment. The document review also revealed that the students being mentored by the organization are actively engaged as the attendance rates for the volunteer attendance programs maintained a robust attendance rate. These high attendance rates signal to investors that the range of program participants are engaged and enthusiastic about the organization, which is an example of the type of data that is needed to attract investors and achieve the organizational goal. High levels of engagement provide private investors with an incentive to engage with the organization's participants and invest in opportunities that might yield a return on investment.

While the document review revealed a proficiency for collecting data, the interviews of the participants revealed a procedural knowledge gap. This gap revealed that the participants were hedged in their current practices and were challenged with collecting additional data and creating additional programming that was specifically aimed at incentivizing private investment in the organization's work. This procedural knowledge gap was congruent to the stakeholder's gap in self-efficacy.

The stakeholders appeared to value the challenge of incentivizing private investment. They expressed challenges in their confidence to implement the protocol changes necessary to achieve the organizational goal. Several stakeholders expressed their desire to create additional programming while simultaneously expressing their doubts in their ability to multi-task the day-to-day work with macro-level implementation.

With no clear organizational mandates or bonus structure, the participants were tasked with creating goals and fulfilling these goals in a silo. This left the stakeholders only being accountable to their goodwill and not a process of growth. As previously asserted in Chapter Three, Bolman and Deal (2010) posit that high performing teams have a system of automatic individual and team accountability. Several participants in this study acknowledged that the level of comfort made for an enjoyable environment, yet was not a growth factor that would get the organization where it sought to grow.

CHAPTER FIVE: SOLUTIONS, IMPLEMENTATIONS AND EVALUATION PLAN

Recommendations for Practice to Address KMO Influences

The findings of this study that were provided in Chapter Four presented an overview of the assumed stakeholder influences according to Clark and Estes' (2008) KMO framework. In this section, the researcher offers recommendations to bridge the knowledge, motivation and organizational influence gaps. Additionally, the researcher offers performance measures for accountability and behaviors that will be helpful to achieve the organizational goal.

Knowledge Influences and Recommendation

The knowledge gap impacting the stakeholder group's ability to meet the organizational performance goal was procedural. While the study group exhibited a conceptual knowledge of the importance of private investment in their initiatives and were reflective about their ability to develop the appropriate programming, the study group did not display a procedural knowledge related to the necessary process of programming and data collection. Table 8 provides a summary of the gap in knowledge influence and the recommendation.

Table 8

Summary of Knowledge Influences and Recommendations

Assumed Knowledge Influence	Principle and Citation	Context-Specific Recommendation
The Board of Directors need to know how to develop programming and assessments that attract private investment. (P)	Effective observational learning is achieved by first organizing and rehearsing modeled behaviors, then enacting them overtly (Mayer, 2011).	Provide training that teaches the stakeholders effective strategies for taking in-depth field notes from each program and comparing these notes to conversations with potential investors.
	Any comprehensive development of programming that attracts	Incorporate modeled examples of how to do this effectively and

private investment will be informed by extensive field notes, in-depth interviews, and explanatory case data that creates a framework for private investor stakeholder collaboration (Wilson et al, 2010)	offer opportunities for practice and feedback.

The knowledge gap identified in the analysis of this study was procedural. These steps will need to be modeled after examples of non-profit initiatives that have successfully incentivized private investment. Effective observational learning is achieved by first organizing and rehearsing modeled behaviors, then enacting them overtly (Mayer, 2011). Any comprehensive development of programming that attracts private investment will be informed by extensive field notes, in-depth interviews, and explanatory case data that creates a framework for private investor stakeholder collaboration (Wilson et al, 2010). In addition to knowing the importance and value of private investment, the Board Members of the Community Cooperative need to know how to implement the collection of data and how to communicate this same data to potential investors. The recommendation then is to provide training that teaches the stakeholders effective strategies for taking in-depth field notes from each program and comparing these notes to conversations with potential investors. By incorporating modeled examples of how to do this effectively and offer opportunities for practice and feedback, the stakeholders will be modeling successful examples of private and non-profit partnerships.

The best method to use in teaching the process of data collection and analysis is training behaviors modeled after successful examples (Clark & Estes, 2008). Being able to meaningfully organize and connect new knowledge to prior knowledge is essential to this process (Schraw & McCrudden, 2006). As previously mentioned in Chapter Two, the Wilson et al. (2010) study employed a comprehensive analysis of social partnerships among a complex network of stakeholder organizations. This quantitative study used field-notes from 33 in-depth interviews and a mix of inductive and deductive reasoning to formulate a conceptual framework and research propositions for a successful private-public social partnership (Wilson et al., 2010). The Loxley (2012) study is also referenced in Chapter Two. Loxley's (2012) research provides an example of how public private partnerships evolved following the global financial crisis of 2008 to meet the needs of municipalities and the surrounding business and social interests. By partnering private interests with value-aligned public organizations and identifying their shared interests in solving problems, Loxley's (2012) research shows that for-profit institutions can solve problems while addressing their desire for positive profit margins. Modeling these examples is consistent with Kirkpatrick's (2006) emphasis on training that focused on results as the metric for success. This literature review supports the recommendation that training the stakeholders and modeling successful examples can effectively address the gap in procedural knowledge.

Motivation Recommendations

The motivation influences identified in Table 9 provide a comprehensive listing of the assumed motivation influence that was validated as a result of this study's completed data collection and analysis. While the assumed influence of value was not validated as a motivation gap, self-efficacy was identified as a motivational gap for the Board of Directors. A stakeholder's mental effort is a key indicator in assessing the motivation of a stakeholder (Clark & Estes, 2008). While the stakeholders that were the subject of this study valued the data gathering process and its ability to incentivize private investment, they did not display a consistent ability to seek and apply new knowledge to the goal of incentivizing private investment.

Table 9

Summary of Motivation Influences and Recommendations

Assumed Motivation Influence*	Principle and Citation	Context-Specific Recommendation
The Board of Directors must believe they can meet the performance goals of obtaining private investment through the relevant tasks that are required to reach performance goals- Self-Efficacy	Creation of a model of best practices based on prior successes will provide a working model as an example of their own capabilities. Internalizing knowledge and then transferring knowledge to colleagues is a hallmark of a healthy work environment that can improve the confidence of colleagues. (Buenaventura-Vera, 2017) Provide instructional support (scaffolding) early on, build in multiple opportunities for practice and gradually remove supports (Pajares, 2006). The impact of leader self-efficacy on the characteristics of work teams. *Intangible Capital*, *13*(4), 824-849.	Create a step-by-step manual for data collection and how it should be gathered. Provide clear lines between the data collection and the investment that is being sought. Include a checklist for the steps so that as each goal is realized the confidence of the stakeholder can grow. Allow these manuals to be living documents that colleagues can review as they also go through the process of data collection.

Approximately 50% of the Board of Directors of the Community Cooperative are not confident in their ability to meet the performance goals of obtaining private investment for non-profit initiatives. In order to close this influence gap, the Board will need to feel competent enough to implement new strategies in governance and administration to meet the performance goals of the Community Cooperative. Motivation, learning and performance are improved when participants in a learning process are confident about their chances for success (Pajares, 2006). This can be accomplished by creation of a model of best practices based on prior successes that will provide Board Members with a working model of an example of their own capabilities.

Internalizing knowledge and then transferring knowledge to colleagues is a hallmark of a healthy work environment that can improve the confidence of colleagues (Buenaventura-Vera, 2017). By creating a step-by-step manual for data collection and how it should be gathered, stakeholders would be provided with clear lines between the data collection and the investment that is being sought. Including a checklist for the steps ensures that each goal that is realized grows the confidence of the stakeholder. These manuals will be living documents that colleagues can review and be confident in as they also go through the process of data collection.

As previously stated in chapter two, the more a person believes that they can achieve a task, the more motivated that person will be to overcome obstacles and achieve the task (Rueda, 2011; Clark & Estes, 2008; Pajares, 2006).). While several factors have an effect on self-efficacy, the research indicates that self-efficacy increases with success and decreases with failure (Pajares, 2006; Rueda, 2011). Once individuals believe that they can create desired outcomes through their work, they can increase their successes and decrease their failures (Bandura, 2000).

Organization Recommendations

Chapter Four revealed that participants experienced gaps in organizational influences. These gaps exposed deficiencies in the organization's ability to support the stakeholders' approach to organizational change. With organizational settings that did not provide adequate accountability to and for the stakeholders, the participants in this study were left without an adequate framework for accomplishing the organizational goal. Table 10 below, identifies the assumed organization influences and the researcher's recommendations.

Table 10

Summary of Organization Influences and Recommendations

Assumed Organization Influence*	Principle and Citation	Context-Specific Recommendation

The Community Cooperative needs resources devoted to the development of data that will incentivize private investment.	Organizations seeking new methods of funding and sustainability will need to invest funding and resources in the development of business strategy and implementation that supports the new funding mechanism (Moizer & Tracey, 2010).	The Community Cooperative should allocate spending resources to hiring a part time employee whose sole function is to collect data and research programming that incentivizes private.
The Community Cooperative needs a structure of shared accountability with private investment related to program performance and data collection.	Non-profit organizations can model best-practices when there are internal accountability measures that ensure the stakeholders are incentivized to work toward a common goal (Costa, Ramus & Andreaus, 2011).	The organization needs to implement accountability measures to ensure that participants work towards the shared organizational goal.

Implement an Incentive into the Plan for Data Collection and Program Creation

According to the interviews with the participants, there are no incentives for collecting data or creating programming that furthers the organizational goals. Implementing incentives for stakeholders creates an atmosphere where adherence to organizational goals are celebrated and rewarded. Incentivized participants who share and communicate with one another will create a work environment that promotes growth (Clark & Estes, 2008). Non-profit organizations can model best-practices when there are internal accountability measures that ensure the stakeholders are incentivized to work toward a common goal (Costa et al., 2011). The organization needs to implement accountability measures to ensure that participants work towards the shared organizational goal.

As stated in chapter 2, Firestone and Riehl (2005) defined accountability as the requirement to account for performance to another by explanation of method and reporting of outcomes. Greller's (2015) theory of accountability asserts that for-profit investment creates an expectation of accountability and measurements for organizational gains. Designing protocols of accountability cannot be overstated. Accountability will also provide a standard of business practice that models how other colleagues and peer organizations respond to the Community Cooperative.

Allocate Resources Devoted to Organizational Goals

The Community Cooperative should devote organizational resources to its goals of incentivizing private investment into its non-profit initiatives. Organizations seeking new methods of funding and sustainability will need to invest funding and resources in the development of business strategy and implementation that supports the new funding mechanism (Moizer & Tracey, 2010). In order to ensure that implementation of the data collection and programming creation plan is effectively executed, the organization should hire a part-time employee to focus all of their efforts on implementation. This role would have the responsibility of collecting all of the data that would be attractive to private investors, such as attendance, demographics, and assessments program participants. Additionally, this part-time employee would be responsible for consulting on the creation of additional programs that would provide a return to investors and fulfill a community need. With a well-defined role, the part-time employee should be able to identify connections between the mentoring and development programs with the needs of potential investors and partners.

Organizations seeking new methods of funding and sustainability will need to invest funding and resources in the development of business strategy and implementation that supports the new funding mechanism (Moizer & Tracey, 2010). While non-profits often invest in expensive fundraisers to incentivize philanthropy, a sustainable practice would involve investing in programs and putting resources into collecting data that incentivize investment and partnership.

Integrated Implementation and Evaluation Plan

The implementation and evaluation framework was informed by the New World Kirkpatrick Model (Kirkpatrick & Kirkpatrick, 2016), which is based on the original Kirkpatrick Four Level Model of Evaluation (Kirkpatrick & Kirkpatrick, 2006). The premise behind this model asserts that evaluation plans start with the organization's goals and works backwards so that the organization's goals, gaps and solutions are more recognizable and aligned with each other. The Kirkpatrick reverse model also allows for the development of solutions that focus on observed conduct, formative learning during the implementation period and signaling of whether the participants are finding success with the implementation strategies. Developing these implementation and evaluation plans will inspire immediate solutions and necessary pivots that will bring the organization closer to achieving the stated goals (Kirkpatrick & Kirkpatrick, 2016).

Organizational Purpose, Need and Expectations

The Community Cooperative for Progressive Action, Inc. (pseudonym-The Community Cooperative) is a non-profit organization dedicated to sustaining the culture that supports and advances the well-being of oppressed peoples in general, and the Pan-African diaspora in particular. To this end, the Community Cooperative works with schools, community organizations, and dedicated city officials to help provide critical education, leadership, and social support programs to youth and young adults in low-income and under-served communities. The Community Cooperative is deeply impacted by its inability to incentivize private investment because the organization currently relies on the donations of its community members, the board, and grant applications. These sources of funding place limitations on the Community Cooperative because grants are often limited to a specific government or foundation initiatives that may not be in alignment with the Community Cooperative's values or goals.

The Community Cooperative's goal will be to develop three programs that incentivize for-profit institutions to invest in non-profit initiatives by the end of 2020. This goal was established in 2019 by the Community Cooperative's Board of Directors. The board set this goal after recognizing the importance of private investment in non-profit initiatives. The theory behind this goal is that for-profit investment creates an expectation of accountability while gifts rarely create accountability measures for organizational or systemic gains (Greller, 2015).

The Board of Directors developed this organizational goal by looking at what progressive steps would be necessary for the organization to scale. While resources were identified as a necessary component of growing the organization, partnerships were identified as the main component to any sustainable growth. The Board determined that for-profit institutions would be better partners than other non-profits who would also compete for grants and funding. They also determined that two programs would not be enough to incentivize private investment. The board also reasoned that creating more than three programs would create management and accountability issues outside of the organization's capacity. Using this reasoning, the Board chose to develop three programs in an effort to incentivize private investment. In order to track progress toward the goal, the Board set three-month and six-month goals for programming initiatives that would align with the organization's overall goal.

The Board of Directors are important to the process of achieving the organization's performance goal because the Board sets the benchmarks for formative assessments that indicate whether the organization is on target to meet its goal. Failure to remain on task and meet each intermediary goal will jeopardize the organization's overall goal to develop programs that incentivize for-profit institutions to invest in their non-profit initiatives by the end of 2020. With the development of effective programs that provide data indicating proficiency in workforce development, social service support, and youth and student programming, the organization would seek to meet with private investors seeking to impact investment in non-profit initiatives. These private investors would be partners in community development, restorative justice and coalition building while also providing examples of the profitability of impact investing.

Level 4: Results and Leading Indicators

Table 11 shows the proposed Level 4: Results and Leading Indicators through outcomes, metrics, and methods for both external and internal outcomes for the Community Cooperative's stakeholder group of Board Members. Based on short-term observations, the metric for success implementation are increased balance sheets, resources for participants and the increased development of the local community.

Table 11

Outcomes, Metrics, and Methods for External and Internal Outcomes

Outcome	Metric(s)	Method(s)
External Outcomes		
Increased Investment In The Community Cooperative's Non-profit programs	Increased Balance Sheet RFP and RFQ procurement of public private partnerships and private partner investment in community development and educational initiatives.	RFP and RFQ partnerships would be tracked by the municipality (NYC) and the balance sheet reported on 990 Filings with the IRS.
Increased Partnership Opportunities	Increase in partners who are aligned in values and who provide resources	Track the number of partners
Increased tax base of community without gentrification	The racial demographics and economic class of the community remaining stable (as tracked by the US census) while the quality of life increases with an increased tax base and allocation of resources proportionate to the needs and desires of the community	Check the updated census and tax records
Internal Outcomes		
Increased participant attendance	Attendance taken at Sessions	sign in and email confirmations at all sessions
Increased resources allocated to programming and community services	Line item budget increased for the funding of programming and community service resources	allocating financial gains from partner investment into the organization

Increased Staff	Number of new staff	Staff data tracked through report to the Board by a part time hire every quarter
Less reliance on Philanthropy	Funding from fundraising decreases compared to funding from private investment Fewer fundraising campaigns	Increased partnerships with private investors

Level 3: Behavior

In order for the organization to experience meaningful change, the stakeholders in the organization will need to exhibit behaviors that further the mission of the organization (Kirkpatrick & Kirkpatrick, 2016). These behaviors will need to be informed by the new information received in training and development. Additionally, these behaviors need to be in alignment with the goals and values of the organization.

Critical Behaviors

The stakeholders of focus are the Board Members of the Community Cooperative. The first critical behavior that must be exhibited by the board is their approval of increased resources to support change. The second critical behavior that must be exhibited by the board is that Board Members must implement accountability measures for one another. The behaviors and how they align with the metric for success, method of success and timing of implementation are in Table 12.

Table 12

Critical Behaviors, Metrics, Methods, and Timing for Evaluation

Critical Behavior	Metric(s)	Method(s)	Timing
Board Members need to approve increased resources to support change	The budget allocation to new initiatives	creating an account that is funded and tracked by the board	within six months
Board Members must implement accountability measures for one another that reward effective communication and penalize communication gaps	incentives and mandates must be tied to new initiatives	writing organizational policy and enforcing the policy	within three months

Board Members must, in unison, create new programs and initiatives that incentivize private investment	programs that are funded by their connection to a funding source or that directly draw funding as a result of the program running	work with for-profit partners to develop training and development that provides needed professional development to a population that can then be sourced for hiring initiatives	within 6 months

Required Drivers

The Community Cooperative's Board will require an organizational setting that reinforces the organizational goal. Mandates and rewards should be established to incentivize the Board as well as hold Board Members accountable if they are engaged in conduct that does not further the organizational goal. The Board Members are the most senior in a non-profit organization, thus, they will be required to drive each other. Table 13 shows the recommended drivers to support critical behaviors of the Board Members.

Table 13

Required Drivers to Support Critical Behaviors

Method(s)	Timing	Critical Behaviors Supported 1, 2, 3 Etc.
Reinforcing		
Participants need a mandate and framework of accountability that enforces adherence to new initiatives that develop programming and collect appropriate data.	Ongoing	1,2
Participants need to invest in the resources necessary to collect data adequately and create programming that will provide data that incentivizes private investment.	Ongoing	1,2
Participants need to hire a part time employee whose sole function is to collect data and research programming that incentivizes private	Ongoing	1,2
Encouraging		
Board Members need to be enthusiastic about the new initiatives and provide adequate resources to staff	Monthly	1,2
Rewarding		
Board Members need to experience a material benefit to their adherence with the organizational goal	Quarterly	1,2
Monitoring		

Board Members need to have formative assessments of their adherence to the organizational goals	Monthly	1,2

Organizational Support

The organization will support the recommendations by implementing strategies that provide resources for the new initiatives as well as provide the accountability for the execution of these new initiatives. The organization needs to implement accountability measures to ensure that Board Members work towards the shared organizational goal of having thirty percent of its budget funded through private investment that fulfills a community need. The level of familiarity and comfort among Board Members within the organization has been helpful as well as harmful to the organizational goals. The organization will need to develop clear language related to expectations and the consequences of missed deadlines. The organization will need to hire a part-time employee who can create timelines that hold the process accountable and also support data tracking. The organization will continue to use non-financial markers of goodwill and good humanity to maintain the value system that inspired the organization from its inception. The organization will balance between its desire to focus on goodwill and humanity with a desire to remain sustainable, viable and scalable.

The organization's support of its programmatic goals are paramount to the success and achievement of the organizational goals. The organization's programmatic goals are to mentor, teach and instruct in the areas of STEM, STEAM, Conflict Resolution, Advocacy, Legal Rights and Food Justice (Gardening, Horticulture, nutrition). Focused in the underserved sections of Brooklyn (East NY, Brownsville, Red Hook, Bed Stuy and Crown Heights), the goal of these programs is to teach communities how to advocate for themselves and become proficient, sustainable and thriving. By providing these instructional and mentoring services, the organization seeks to spark community development coming from within the community instead of from real estate and banking professionals.

Level 2: Learning

A crucial step towards closing the assumed influence gaps will include stakeholder learning goals. These learning steps will be aimed at the stakeholders' abilities to collect data and create programming that incentivize private investment. Additionally, stakeholders will learn the importance of accountability measures that are necessary to accomplishing organizational goals.

Learning Goals

After the completion of the solutions recommended by the researcher, the stakeholders will be able to:

1. Apply steps to create programming and data collection protocols that incentivize private investment (Procedural).

2. Allocate organizational support for organizational goals (Procedural).

3. Understand and execute the stated goal of the organization (Confidence- Self-efficacy).

4. Feel positive about new organizational goals that will render the organization more sustainable (Mood).

5. Seek organizational support in developing accountability measures that inspire board member responsibility without sending a chilling effect throughout the organization (P).

Program

The Learning goals identified in the previous section can be accomplished with a training program that emphasizes reflection, process and execution. The Board Members will learn about modeling behavior, corporate governance and budgeting. The training will be delivered over the course of four weeks with one session per week for four hours a day. The training will be conducted by Community Resource Exchange (CRE).

The program will be run virtually through a zoom conference. Materials will be provided by email at least 48 hours before each class. The program will focus on the organizational goals and information and examples of organizations that have successfully achieved similar goals. These modeled examples will serve as a template for how the Board Members can begin to implement the changes needed for the sustainability of the organization.

Evaluation of the Components of Learning

A key component of learning is confidence. Learners of new methods of implementation need to believe that they can apply their new knowledge in practice. Evaluating the effectiveness of a training is best accomplished by evaluating the declarative and procedural knowledge methods of the training. Table 14 describes the evaluation methods and timing associated with the guidelines for learning.

Table 14

Evaluation of the Components of Learning for the Program

Method(s) or Activity(ies)	Timing
Declarative Knowledge "I know it."	
Knowledge checks at each stage of the implementation plan	Weekly meetings
Knowledge checks through small group meetings among stakeholders	Monthly meetings
Procedural Skills "I can do it right now."	
Application of the skills to develop programming that incentivizes private investment	Monthly meetings
Application of the skills to collect data that incentivizes private investment	Monthly meetings
Attitude "I believe this is worthwhile."	

Board Member assessment-	Every Three Months
Observing Board Member Attitudes during sessions	At weekly check ins and Monthly check ins
Confidence "I think I can do it on the job."	
Board Member Self-Efficacy assessment	Every Three Months
Commitment "I will do it on the job."	
Create a sub-committee on the Board responsible for the action plan and Board Member accountability	Initial Meeting

Level 1: Reaction

Table 15 provides a formative and summative approach to evaluate Board engagement and implementation (Kirkpatrick & Kirkpatrick, 2016). The evaluation methods include program observations and Board member check-ins (Kirkpatrick & Kirkpatrick, 2016).

Table 15

Components to Measure Reactions to the Program

Method(s) or Tool(s)	Timing
Engagement	
Evaluation of Engagement and Training	Monthly
Relevance	
Evaluation of participants	Weekly
Customer Satisfaction	
Evaluation of Board's approval/disapproval of training	Monthly

Evaluation Tools

Immediately Following the Program Implementation

The participants will be evaluated during the training in order to determine the effectiveness of the training and to monitor how participants are feeling about the training. This evaluation will be used to measure the relevance and participants' immediate satisfaction with the program implementation. By providing a measure of the Level 1 reaction to training and implementation, the participants will help ensure that the organization reaches its goals. In addition to the Level 1 measure, this evaluation will also inform the Level 2 measure of learning.

Specifically, the participants will be evaluated on how the training is developing their knowledge, skills, attitude and confidence. Participants will be given a survey in an effort to deliver the most accurate feedback. The questions and responses will be anonymous so that participants can offer unencumbered questions and elicit comprehensive responses. The questions and answers, without other identifying information, will be available for the training staff to see during the training period so that the feedback is in real-time and pivots can be made quickly. See Appendix C for this evaluation.

Delayed for a Period After the Program Implementation

At the conclusion of the initial training of participants, the participants will begin the work of data collection and program creation that incentivize private investment. After thirty days of working at the stated task, the participants will have an opportunity to complete a survey to determine the effectiveness of the training and how the training is being implemented in the field. The timing of this evaluation will take place after thirty days so that participants can provide formative feedback that is informed by the participants' training, experiences and reflection. This evaluation instrument will measure reaction, learning, behavior and organizational results. Measuring all four levels will provide information on the relevance of the training as well as participant satisfaction, knowledge, skills, attitude, confidence and behaviors. The Level 3 measure is particularly important as the behaviors of the participants should be informed by the training and will be the leading indicator of whether the organization achieves its desired outcomes, see Appendix D for this evaluation.

Data Analysis and Reporting

The Level Four goal for Board Members is to have a robust and sustainable organization that maintains its non-profit purpose while yielding private investment in its non-profit initiatives.

When this goal is achieved, the organization will increase its balance sheets, resources for participants, and participate in the increased development of the local community. The members of the board will pull data from the organization and provide surveys to the organization's constituents to understand priority items and what areas need additional support. The Board Members will then use this data to determine what community needs can be met while providing data that would incentivize private investment. In order to accomplish this, the Board Members will also provide a survey to potential investors to better understand what investors are looking for as an impact investment return.

Table 16 exemplifies the measurement for impact.

Table 16

Organizational Goals

Goal	Target	Actual	Gap
Increase balance sheet	$150,000 in investment income	TBD	TBD
Increase in Asset capture	$25,000	TBD	TBD

Summary

With a well-developed protocol for accountability and data collection methods, the Community Cooperative can achieve its organizational goals and remain sustainable. This study used the New World Kirkpatrick Model to plan the training and focus on the end goal. By constructing the evaluation and participant training backwards from long-term impact to short-term impact, the researcher was able to remain focused on the overall goals of the organization and while working through the critical behaviors of the Board Members. By providing formative assessments throughout a summative evaluation, the researcher maintained an alignment between organization and stakeholder goals.

Limitations

The inability to verify the veracity of each response provided a limitation to the interview responses. In an attempt to evade response biases, the researcher posed interview questions that were confirmed by follow up questions that were designed to elicit accurate responses. The accuracy of the responses has helped to create an atmosphere of reflection, growth and development.

Another limitation was the role that the researcher maintains within the Community Cooperative. As a board member, the researcher's role could have influenced the other board member's responses. However, because the researcher does not have a leadership or hierarchical relationship to any of the other Board Members, this bias was excluded. Additionally, each board member volunteered for this study after a conversation with the researcher and an affirmation that this study was designed as an evaluation of how the organization could operate more effectively.

The focus of this study was limited to one non-profit organization and this presented an additional limitation to this study. A comprehensive evaluation of the stakeholders in other organizations would have provided a more in-depth perspective of the challenges presented with incentivizing private investment in non-profit initiatives. A triangulated view of the knowledge, motivation and organizational influences could offer a more whole perspective on the field of impact investing and gaps that may exist in the field of study. The researcher attempted to solve for this limitation by providing a comprehensive review of the field in the literature review section of this study.

An additional limitation in this study was presented by unforeseen circumstances that deeply impacted the stakeholders as well as the organization. During the data collection phase of this study, the global pandemic of COVID-19, caused a global shift in resources, priorities and agendas. The effect of of COVID-19 on the world cannot be overstated. The world may not truly know the complete effect that this pandemic has caused and how its resulting traumas may show up, however, the researcher asserts that the interview results present stakeholders answering questions about behaviors and conduct through the lens of active trauma. As a result, all data collection for this study was done as participants may have been going through active trauma that presented in unforeseen ways. Specifically, the findings in the study found that participants were not confidant and were not knowledgeable about procedure. However, the global trauma of COVID-19 and the abusive news cycle may have contributed to this lack of confidence and lack of procedural knowledge.

Implications for Practice

Traditionally, non-profit organizations would rely on donations in order to fulfill their missions of societal change or improvement. This study explored the opportunity for private investment to have a profound effect on the framework for non-profit funding. By relying on investment that is tied to a social good, non-profits can become viable and sustainable organizations that are not relegated to asking for donations to improve society. Instead, non-profit organizations can incentivize investment by providing returns to investors that rival traditional investments. This revolutionizes the non-profit space and develops a model of sustainable profit building for investors and sustainable community building for non-profit organizations. As previously stated in Chapter One, a successful example of a non-profit and for-profit partnership providing profitability and social good occurred in the Trelstad and Katz (2011) research where malaria nets were developed to stop disease. In this research, a non-profit entity partnered with a for-profit company to provide malaria nets during an outbreak of malaria (Trelstad & Katz, 2011).

This partnership ended the malaria outbreak and provided a profit boon to the for-profit entity (Trelstad & Katz, 2011).

Future Research

Future research should include a field-study of impact investment and how it continues to compare to traditional investment tools. The literature in this study examined private investment in non-profit initiatives. However, a future study should examine private investment in non-profit institutions as a more robust model for growth. The implications of this research could reveal why for-profit investment in institutions might be instructive as a business model for non-profits. Alternatively, the research could reveal the misalignment in values between non-profits and for-profit institutions and substantiate why non-profits and for-profit institutions should remain at an arm's length away from each other.

Conclusions

This dissertation addressed the need to incentivize private investment in non-profit initiatives and the challenge of finding shared common goals when private institutions support non-profit entities. While the concept of private investment in non-profit initiatives creates a unique opportunity for non-profit entities to offer a return on investment that is not limited to an interest rate, the evidence shows that positive social impact and other non-profit outcomes are not enough to incentivize private investment in non-profit and government work (Shaoul et al, 2011). This study sought to examine the shared values that non-profit organizations might have with for profit institutions and how they might work together to accomplish congruent goals. The researcher used the Community Cooperative as a case study and interviewed the board member stakeholder group to evaluate the organization's ability to incentivize private investment in its non-profit initiatives. The Community Cooperative developed organizational goals to incentivize private investment in its non-profit initiatives and identified that increased data collection and programming would be required to accomplish this goal.

Using the KMO framework from Clark and Estes (2008), the researcher identified and evaluated the knowledge, motivation and organizational gaps that serve as barriers to the organizational goal of incentivizing private investment in its non-profit initiatives. The stakeholder group of study was interviewed and documents were collected from the organization. Following the stakeholder interviews, the researcher determined that the stakeholder group had gaps in procedural knowledge, self-efficacy and that the organizational setting did not provide enough stakeholder accountability. As a result of the findings in chapter four, the researcher recommended training the stakeholders to collect data, communicate accountability methods and implement accountability methods. With the proper training and organizational modeling, the stakeholders can develop practices that allow the organization and the stakeholders to accomplish their goals.

References

Aulgur, J. J. (2016). Governance and board member identity in an emerging nonprofit organization. *Administrative Issues Journal: Connecting Education, Practice, and Research, 6*(1), 6-21.

Akhtar, S., Ghayas, S., & Adil, A. (2013). Self-efficacy and optimism as predictors of organizational commitment among bank employees. *International Journal of Research Studies in Psychology, 2*(2), 33-42.

Al-Tabbaa, O., Gadd, K., & Ankrah, S. (2013). Excellence models in the non-profit context: strategies for continuous improvement. *International Journal of Quality & Reliability Management, 30*(5), 590-612.

Arrow, K. J., Dasgupta, P., Goulder, L. H., Mumford, K. J., & Oleson, K. (2012). Sustainability and the measurement of wealth. *Environment and Development Economics, 17*(3), 317-353.

Assembly, G. (2015). Sustainable development goals. *SDGs, Transforming our world: the, 2030.*

Bear, S., Rahman, N., & Post, C. (2010). The impact of board diversity and gender composition on corporate social responsibility and firm reputation. *Journal of Business Ethics, 97*(2), 207-221.

Bhattacharya, A., Oppenheim, J., & Stern, N. (2015). Driving sustainable development through better infrastructure: Key elements of a transformation program. *Brookings Global Working Paper Series.*

Blery, E. K., Katseli, E., & Tsara, N. (2010). Marketing for a non-profit

organization. *International Review on Public and Nonprofit Marketing, 7*(1), 57-68.

Brest, P., & Born, K. (2013). When can impact investing create real impact. *Stanford Social*

Innovation Review, 11(4), 22-31.Cimera, R. E., & Cowan, R. J. (2009). The costs of

services

and employment outcomes achieved by adults with autism in the US. *Autism, 13*(3), 285-

302.

Brinkerhoff, D. W., & Brinkerhoff, J. M. (2011). Public-private partnerships: Perspectives on

purposes, publicness, and good governance. *Public Administration and*

Development,31(1), 2-14.

Bugg-Levine, A., & Emerson, J. (2011). Impact Investing: Transforming How We Make

Money while Making a Difference. *Innovations: Technology, Governance,*

Globalization,6(3), 9-18.

Cairns, B., Harris, M., Hutchison, R., & Tricker, M. (2005). Improving performance? The

adoption and implementation of quality systems in UK nonprofits. *Nonprofit*

Management

and Leadership, 16(2), 135-151.

Carnochan, S., Samples, M., Myers, M., & Austin, M. J. (2014). Performance measurement

challenges in nonprofit human service organizations. *Nonprofit and Voluntary Sector*

Quarterly, 43(6), 1014-1032.

Cingano, F. (2014). Trends in income inequality and its impact on economic growth.

Clark, R. E., & Estes, F. (2008). *Turning research into results: A guide to selecting the right*

performance solutions. CEP Press.

Clark, G. L., Feiner, A., & Viehs, M. (2015). From the stockholder to the stakeholder: How

    sustainability can drive financial outperformance. *Available at SSRN 2508281*.

Chowdhry, B., Davies, S. W., & Waters, B. (2014, May). Incentivizing impact investing.

    In *Conference on the Impact of Responsible and Sustainable Investing*, Hong Kong

    University of Science and Technology.

Cowen, T. (2011). *The great stagnation: How America ate all the low-hanging fruit of modern*

    history, got sick, and will (eventually) feel better: A Penguin eSpecial from Dutton.

Penguin.

Engel, E., Fischer, R., & Galetovic, A. (2013). The basic public finance of public–private.

    partnerships. *Journal of the European Economic Association*, *11*(1), 83-111.

Eisinger, P. (2002). Organizational capacity and organizational effectiveness among street-level

    food assistance programs. *Nonprofit and Voluntary Sector Quarterly*, *31*(1), 115-130.

Feldman, M., Hadjimichael, T., Lanahan, L., & Kemeny, T. (2016). The logic of economic

    development: a definition and model for investment. *Environment and Planning C:*

    Government and Policy, *34*(1), 5-21.

Fichtner, J. (2014). Privateers of the Caribbean: The hedge funds–US–UK–offshore

    nexus. *Competition & Change*, *18*(1), 37-53.

Forrer, J., Kee, J. E., Newcomer, K. E., & Boyer, E. (2010). Public–private partnerships and

    the public accountability question. *Public Administration Review*, *70*(3), 475-484.

Glesne, C. (2011). Chapter 6: But is it ethical? Considering what is right. *Becoming qualitative*

    researchers: An introduction, *4*, 162-183.

Gordon, R. H. (2010). Public finance and economic development: reflections based on

    experience in China. *Journal of Globalization and Development*, *1*(1).

Grabenwarter, Uli and Liechtenstein, Heinrich, In Search of Gamma – An Unconventional

    Perspective on Impact Investing (November 25, 2011). *IESE Business School Working*

    Paper. doi: 10.2139/ssrn.2120040.

Greller, M. (2015). Leasehold: An institutional framework for understanding nonprofit

    governance in a civil society context. *Administrative Sciences, 5*(3), 165-176.

Gutiérrez, G., & Philippon, T. (2017). *Declining Competition and Investment in the US* (No.

    w23583). National Bureau of Economic Research.

Hacke, R., Wood, D., & Urquilla, M. (2015). Community investment: Focusing on the

    system. *The Kresge Foundation.*

Hanleybrown, F., Kania, J., & Kramer, M. (2012). Channeling change: Making collective

    impact work. *Stanford Social Innovation Review.*

Herman, R. D., & Renz, D. O. (2008). Advancing nonprofit organizational effectiveness research

    and theory: Nine theses. *Nonprofit management and leadership, 18*(4), 399-415.

Hess, J., & Bacigalupo, A. (2013). Applying emotional intelligence skills to leadership and

    decision making in non-profit organizations. *Administrative Sciences, 3*(4), 202-220.

Hum, T. (2010). Planning in Neighborhoods with Multiple Publics: Opportunities and

    Challenges for Community-Based Nonprofit Organizations. *Journal of Planning*

    Education and Research, 29(4), 461-477. doi:10.1177/0739456x10368700.

Edward T. Jackson (2013) Interrogating the theory of change: evaluating impact investing where

    it matters most, *Journal of Sustainable Finance & Investment*, 3:2, 95-

    110, doi: 10.1080/20430795.2013.776257

Kimberlin, S. E. (2010). Advocacy by nonprofits: Roles and practices of core advocacy

    organizations and direct service agencies. *Journal of Policy Practice, 9*(3-4), 164-182

Kharas, H., & McArthur, J. (2014). Mobilizing private investment for post-2015 sustainable development. *Brookings Briefing Note. Washington DC.*

Klijn, E. H., & Koppenjan, J. (2016). The impact of contract characteristics on the performance of public–private partnerships (PPPs). *Public Money & Management*, *36*(6), 455-462.

Lecy, J. D., Schmitz, H. P., & Swedlund, H. (2012). Non-governmental and not-for-profit organizational effectiveness: A modern synthesis. *Voluntas: International Journal of Voluntary and Nonprofit Organizations*, *23*(2), 434-457.

Loxley, J. (2012). Public-private partnerships after the global financial crisis: Ideology trumping economic reality. *Studies in Political Economy*, *89*(1), 7-38.

Lukes, M., & Stephan, U. (2012). Nonprofit leaders and for-profit entrepreneurs: Similar people with different motivation. *Ceskoslovenska psychologie*, *56*(1), 41-55.

Metrick, A., & Yasuda, A. (2011). Venture capital and other private equity: a survey. *European Financial Management*, *17*(4), 619-654.

McMurray, A. J., Pirola-Merlo, A., Sarros, J. C., & Islam, M. M. (2010). Leadership, climate, psychological capital, commitment, and wellbeing in a non-profit organization. *Leadership & Organization Development Journal*, *31*(5), 436-457.

Milligan, K., & Schöning, M. (2011). Taking a realistic approach to impact investing: observations from the world economic forum's global agenda council on social innovation. *Innovations: Technology, Governance, Globalization*, *6*(3), 155-166.

Papineau, D., & Kiely, M. C. (1996). Participatory evaluation in a community organization: Fostering stakeholder empowerment and utilization. *Evaluation and program planning*, *19*(1), 79-93.

Ragin, L., & Palandjian, T. (2013). Social impact bonds: Using impact investment to expand effective social programs. *Community Development Investment Review*, *9*(1), 63-67.

Rangan, V. K., Appleby, S., & Moon, L. (2011). The promise of impact investing. *Harvard Business School, Background Note*.

Robinson, T. (1996). Inner-city innovator: the non-profit community development corporation. *Urban Studies*, *33*(9), 1647-1670.

Brown, R. T., & Fields, D. (2011). Leaders engaged in self-leadership: Can followers tell the difference?. *Leadership*, *7*(3), 275-293.

Roundy, Philip and Holzhauer, Hunter and Dai, Ye, Finance or Philanthropy? Exploring the Motivations and Criteria of Impact Investors (February 4, 2017). *Social Responsibility Journal*, Forthcoming. Retrieved from https://ssrn.com/abstract=2911570

Shaoul, J., Stafford, A., & Stapleton, P. (2011). Private finance: Bridging the gap for the UK's

Dartford and Skye bridges? *Public Money and Management*, *31*(1), 51-58. doi: 10.1080/09540962.2011.545547

Schein, E.H. (2017*). Organizational culture and leadership*, 5th Edition. San Francisco: JosseyBass.

Shinwell, M., & Shamir, E. (2018). Measuring the impact of businesses on people's well-being and sustainability.

Soederberg, S. (2009), *Corporate power and ownership in contemporary capitalism: the politics of resistance and domination*. Routledge.

Trelstad, B., & Katz, R. (2011). Mission, Margin, Mandate: Multiple Paths to Scale. *Innovations: Technology, Governance, Globalization,6*(3), 41-

53. doi:10.1162/inov_a_00081

Mildred E. Warner (2013) Private finance for public goods: social impact bonds. *Journal of Economic Policy Reform,* 16:4, 303-319.

David Wood, Ben Thornley & Katie Grace (2013) Institutional impact investing: practice and policy, *Journal of Sustainable Finance & Investment*, 3(2), 75-94, doi: 10.1080/20430795.2013.776256

Department of Developmental Services. (2008). *Fact book.* Retrieved from http://www.dds.ca.gov/FactsStats/docs/factbook_11th.pdf

Wójcik, D., Knight, E., O'Neill, P., & Pažitka, V. (2018). Economic geography of investment banking since 2008: The geography of shrinkage and shift. *Economic Geography, 94*(4), 376-399.

APPENDICES

Appendix A

Research Questions:
1. What are the Board of Director's knowledge and motivation related to incentivizing private investment in non-profit initiatives?
2. What is the interaction between organizational culture and context and Board of Directors' knowledge and motivation to increase private investment in non-profit initiatives?
3. What are the recommendations for organizational practice in the areas of knowledge, motivation and organizational resources related to private investment into non-profit initiatives?

KMO Influence	Interview Question
Knowledge Influences	
The Board of Directors need to understand what factors incentivize private investors to invest in non-profit initiative	
	What are some things that might negatively influence an investors desire to invest in non-profit initiatives?
	Describe how private investors determine which non-profit initiatives to invest in, if any?
The Board of Directors need to know how to develop programming and assessments that attract private investment	What are some metrics private investors look for when deciding what to invest in?
	What are some desired outcomes for private investors when deciding what to invest in?
	What programs, if any, do investors look for when deciding what to invest in?
The Board of Directors need to reflect on their ability to	What has been your experience with developing programs that incentivize private investment?

develop proficiency in program development and data collection	What have you observed about the process of collecting data that informs private investment?
	Have you observed improvements in program development and data collection that have helped support investment efforts?
	Describe areas in which you would seek growth in your ability to explain programs and in a manner that will attract private investors
Motivation Influences	
The Board of Directors need to value private investment into non-profit initiatives	Why is it important for non-profits initiatives to receive private investment?
	Are there any detriments to non-profit initiatives receiving private investment?
	What has been your experience with private investment in non-profit initiatives?
The Board of Directors need to believe they can meet the performance goals of obtaining private investment through the relevant tasks that are required to reach performance goals.	Describe your proficiency in programming and data collection.
	Describe what limits your ability to develop programming and data that incentivizes private investment.
Organization Influences	
The Community Cooperative needs clearly defined goals that are communicated to potential investors.	What are your organization's goals for the next ten years?
	How does your organization communicate its' goals to participants?

	Describe 3-5 ways in which your organization can improve how it communicates its goals to participants.

The Community Cooperative needs resources devoted to the development of data that will incentivize private investment.	What influences the allocation of organizational resources devoted to programming that serves the community need and incentivizes private investment in its non-profit initiatives?
	Does the Community Cooperative have sufficient trained personnel capable of conducting data collection and analysis that will provide the appropriate data that will attract private investors?
	What data does the organization use to incentivize private investment?
The Community Cooperative needs a structure of shared accountability with private investment related to program performance and data collection.	What organizational mandates exist to ensure that data is collected that incentivizes private investment?
	What consequences exist for when data is not collected in accordance with organizational goals?
	What benefits or bonuses exist for participants who collect data that incentivizes private investment?

Appendix B

Questions: Which KMO influences will be examined through Document Analysis?

KMO Influence	Document Analysis
Knowledge Influences	
The Board of Directors need to understand what factors incentivize private investors to invest in non-profit initiative	
The Board of Directors need to know how to develop programming and assessments that attract private investment	
The Board of Directors need to reflect on their ability to develop proficiency in program development and data collection	X- Assessments of programming from participants
Motivation Influences	
The Board of Directors need to value private investment into non-profit initiatives	X- A review of Tax credits available to private investors
The Board of Directors need to believe they can meet the performance goals of obtaining private investment through the relevant tasks that are required to reach performance goals.	
Organization Influences	

The Community Cooperative needs resources devoted to the development of data that will incentivize private investment.	

The Community Cooperative needs a structure of accountability related to data collection and its connection to private investment.	
The Community Cooperative needs clearly defined goals that are communicated to participants.	

Appendix C

Evaluation Instrument: Immediate

KNOWLEDGE
1. My understanding of data collection and how it corresponds to private investment as presented in the current training can be best described as:
A. Clearly Understood B. Partially Understood C. Barely Understood D. Not Understood

SKILLS
2. I am now able to collect data and create programming that incentivizes private investment. This statement is:
   A. True   B. False

ATTITUDE
3. This training and the work I am being prepared for is important. This statement is:
   A. True   B. False
      (if false, please provide a brief explanation)

CONFIDENCE
4. My level of confidence during the training is:
   A. High B. Medium C. Low

RELEVANCE
5. The training that I am receiving is relevant for the work that I am tasked to perform. This statement is:
   A. True B. False
      (if false, please provide a brief explanation)

SATISFACTION
6. My level of satisfaction with the quality of the programming provided in the training is:
   A. High B. Medium C. Low

Appendix D

Evaluation Instrument: Delayed

LEVEL 1

REACTION

1. The training adequately prepared me for the work of data collection and program creation that incentivizes private investment. This statement is:
   A. True B. False
      (if false, please provide a brief explanation)

RELEVANCE

2. I am very satisfied with the relevance of the material presented in the training and how it relates to the work I am conducting in the field. This statement is:
   B. True B. False
      (if false, please provide a brief explanation)

SATISFACTION

3. I am very satisfied with the quality of the material presented in the training and how it relates to the work I am conducting in the field. This statement is:
   C. True B. False
         (if false, please provide a brief explanation)

LEVEL 2

KNOWLEDGE

4. My understanding of data collection and how it corresponds to private investment as presented in the current training can be best described as:
   B. Clearly Understood B. Partially Understood C. Barely Understood D. Not Understood

SKILLS

5. I am now able to collect data and create programming that incentivizes private investment. This statement is:
   B. True   B. False

ATTITUDE

6. This training and the work I am being prepared for is important. This statement is:
   B. True   B. False
      (if false, please provide a brief explanation)

CONFIDENCE

7. My level of confidence during the training is:
   B. High B. Medium C. Low

LEVEL 3

BEHAVIOR

8. As a result of the training, I am committing to accountability and the process of efficient data collection. This statement is:
A. True   B. False
(if false, please provide a brief explanation)

9. The training provided helped me develop new skills in budgeting, team-building, accountability and the development of data designed to incentivize private investment. This statement is:
B. True   B. False
(if false, please provide a brief explanation)

10. I received appropriate information on the processes of change occurring in my work environment and the need for change, despite its short-term difficulties.
A. Strongly agree B. Moderately agree C. Moderately disagree D. Strongly disagree
11. I received appropriate information on practical self-care activities that I can repeat as my schedule permits to help reduce my stress and maintain my sense of identity.
A. Strongly agree B. Moderately agree C. Moderately disagree D. Strongly disagree
12. I received training and education to advance my appreciation and acknowledgement of the challenges and benefits of teaching on-ground and online.
Strongly agree B. Moderately agree C. Moderately disagree D. Strongly disagree

LEVEL 4

RESULTS

11. As a result of the training, I am collecting data and creating programming that incentivized private investment in my organization's non-profit initiatives. This statement is:
A. True B. False
(if false, please provide a brief explanation)